# Heart Magick

*By the same author:*

Wicca: A Modern Guide to Witchcraft & Magick

The Harmony Tarot: A Deck for Healing and Growth

# Heart Magick

## WICCAN RITUALS FOR SELF-LOVE + SELF-CARE

### HARMONY NICE

This publication is designed to provide accurate and authoritative information in regard to the subject matter covered. It is sold with the understanding that the publisher is not engaged in rendering legal, accounting, or other professional service. If legal advice or other expert assistance is required, the services of a competent professional person should be sought. —*From a Declaration of Principles Jointly Adopted by a Committee of the American Bar Association and a Committee of Publishers and Associations*

Published by Sourcebooks
P.O. Box 4410, Naperville, Illinois 60567-4410
(630) 961-3900
sourcebooks.com

Originally published in 2022 in Great Britain by Rider, an imprint of Ebury Publishing. Rider is part of the Penguin Random House group of companies whose addresses can be found at global.penguinrandomhouse.com

Cataloging-in-Publication Data is on file with the Library of Congress.

Printed and bound in the United States of America.
SB 10 9 8 7 6 5 4 3 2 1

**Please note:**
Fire can be very unpredictable. If you are carrying out a practice that uses fire in any form – such as candles, incense or using smoke – always work away from draughts and hanging fabrics. If you are outdoors, perform your rituals away from overhanging plants and trees. Use fire-proof containers and never leave flames to burn unattended. It is advised that professional medical advice is obtained for specific health matters and before changing any medication or dosage. Neither the publisher nor the author accepts any legal responsibility for any personal injury or other damage or loss arising from the use of information in this book.

This book is dedicated to the special moments that come after healing. The ability to stop and watch the birds speak to each other. To tasting the magick in coffee. To feeling safe with the people you love, to the quiet sound of your breath during meditation. To following your dreams at last; to saying no, to saying yes, to moving away, to taking breaks, and to finally feeling alive again.

Above all, it is dedicated to the endless possibility we all have to grow life, wherever we go, and whoever we become.

*'Today I will remind myself, again, of how much I am loved.'*

# Contents

# Introduction:

# My Story and the Making of this Book

Throughout my life, Wicca has brought me positive experiences. I have always been fascinated with fantasy and magick, and I began practising witchcraft at the age of fourteen. Then, at the age of seventeen, I found a Scott Cunningham book in a local shop and the Wiccan faith was brought to my attention. At that time, I was in a period of deep depression and my self-perception was extremely negative. But when I discovered Wicca, I became aware of the many layers of human consciousness.

Looking back now, I would say that this was the first time that I went through a period of real self-awareness. I was thinking more and more about how my actions affected others and the steps that I was taking which led to negative outcomes. I became conscious of how I played a part in this world, and how I could extend my relationship with the universe. I wanted to learn and I was curious about things within spirituality and Wicca that were related to nature, such as the fae or fairy folk, vibrational energy and divination.

I also read Wiccan discussions about the vibrational connections between beings, and I realised how this applied to my life. For example, when I was a child, I was convinced that I could hear the trees talk (yes, slightly concerning, I know!), but it wasn't a voice – more of a vibration. After learning about the concept that everything has vibrational energy, some of the doubts that I had about my experiences disappeared, and my belief that there is magick everywhere in this world was affirmed. I started to understand that I simply needed to look for it.

For a wonderful couple of years, I enjoyed the process of delving into Wicca. I wanted to cast every spell, learn about every herb, and I felt my connection with the earth strengthen significantly. I found manifestation almost effortless, and I felt happy and healthy in my body. I developed an online career, creating videos educating others on the Wiccan faith, which kept me learning and engaging in the craft.

But unfortunately something had gradually been building in my subconscious that shifted my path. Around the age of nineteen, I experienced an assault that left me very shaken. I can see now that from this point on I started to lose my strength. Without consciously realising it, I began to spiral downwards, slowly at first and then it seemed to gather momentum. I was constantly trying to solve my problems with the same answers and failed to learn from my mistakes. When that didn't work, I turned to perfecting my outward appearance. When that didn't work either, I turned to alcohol. Unfortunately, trauma had begun to feel normal to me, and I ignored most of my intuition and pain; I came not to trust it and buried my instincts instead.

This lifestyle and mindset inevitably left me feeling detached from my Wiccan path, as I struggled to connect with myself and the earth. Spells increasingly felt almost impossible, and I lacked enthusiasm for anything that didn't instantly give me a feeling of validation. Then, in 2020, the pandemic hit us all. For the first time in a long time, I was forced to stop moving, to sit still and re-evaluate everything. As many people may know, after years of living in survival mode, any unprocessed feelings or trauma can suddenly hit you like a ton of bricks. I found it really difficult to muster up the energy to work, so I took a break from my job as a YouTuber and from social media. I think that was such a confusing time for all of us. I spent my days going for walks and I started to spend periods of time every day just sitting and thinking, even if only for around ten minutes or so. I found that I got something positive from this stillness, and I began to research and practise meditation.

Following months of reflection and meditating, I could see that my recent Wiccan path had become less about the nature and beauty of the world and more about keeping up with *identifying* as spiritual, rather than actually being spiritual. My practice felt as though it had become a task, with its main purpose being to maintain an image for social media. I had completely lost any of the fire that I once had inside me. My intuition had faded, along with any drive that I had for living beyond just pretending to be happy. I put these feelings and thoughts down to many causes, including unhealthy relationships that had drained my inner trust and a fear of failure and of genuine happiness. I realised why there was a wall between myself and my spirituality. I kept asking myself, 'How can I practise a religion based on intuition when I have no idea of what I need?'

I looked into Buddhism, Quakerism and Taoism, all of which have beautiful philosophies and interesting ideas about life and death, which helped me along with my journey. Inevitably, though, this research brought me back to Wicca – this time with a beginner's approach. It became clear that what I needed most was to regain the joy that I had found earlier in my practice.

I craved simplicity, self-discovery, and new knowledge. It became more evident when I wanted to perform rituals that I needed to be patient and rest at other times. My altar became a small table with a single candle, a plant and a statue representing Mother Nature. I stopped forcing myself to be perfect and became the joyful witch of my heart instead. It almost felt as though I was restarting my spiritual journey, even though the path was within a religion that I had followed for many years. So I started to take a mindful approach to Wicca and applied this to areas of my life that I had never considered when I entered the faith in my teens.

## WHAT IS THIS BOOK ABOUT?

This book will take you on a healing journey. It won't offer you quick fixes, but show you a beautiful way of being that can help you connect with natural forces and change your life. I didn't want to write a self-help book that offers inauthentic instructions about what to do to become happy. Nor did I want to influence anyone into spending money and time buying crystals and acquiring other possessions for magickal purposes, without emphasising that the most important things you need are already within you.

When I entered the faith at a young age, it felt like a very action-based religion and, in some ways, it is. But in other respects, I've learnt that we truly have nothing if we don't take care of our minds. I have written this book based on my personal experience, combined with knowledge about the faith that I wanted to share and the ways that it can add to your life and assist your wellbeing with a mindful approach. While my first book, *Wicca*, is an introduction to the faith, this book explains how you can put your knowledge into practice and use witchcraft to improve your relationship with the world around you and, most importantly, yourself, whether you are new to Wicca or an experienced witch. I want to take you through essential aspects of the foundation of what the Wiccan religion can give to you and how you can use it to help yourself create positive energy in all areas of your life.

The book is structured in four main parts:

**Part 1: Magick for the Mind** explains the importance of intuition and self-trust in magick. It introduces the life-changing power of meditation and shows how this can be a way to connect with your inner child and shadow self – hidden aspects of yourself that may influence your magickal intentions. It then encourages you to express yourself creatively through art magick.

**Part 2: Magick for the Body** picks up where Part 1 leaves off by showing how we can nourish ourselves magickally through food and drink. It describes how both magickal movement and rest form part of a harmonious, balanced magickal lifestyle, and touches upon the subject of magick in physical relationships.

**Part 3: Magick for the Soul** suggests ways in which Wicca can offer a personal path towards self-understanding and celebration through the festivals of the year. It describes how to make a self-love altar and to live by the Rede, which describes the Wiccan belief system. It also considers the value of healing and letting go.

**Part 4: Magick for the World** is all about expressing ourselves and our desires in the world, finding our tribe and connecting with nature. It also looks at the role of magickal protection and cleansing to keep ourselves safe from negative people and harmful forces as part of our self-care on our journey through life.

## HOW TO USE THIS BOOK

This book will be useful if you are curious about taking a different approach to practising Wicca or maybe you feel stuck in your faith. Throughout the chapters, I will be sharing the rituals that helped me on my journey. You don't have to perform the spells in sequence while reading, but can read ahead or refer back to them in times of need.

I encourage you to use this book in any way that works for you, whether it is simply for finding ideas on how to boost your wellbeing and happiness, or approaching your craft in a more mindful way. I believe that witchcraft and Wicca and the process you apply to the craft is individual to each person. I spent years trying to live up to everyone's expectation of what a witch should be, so this book is written from the perspective of no longer wanting to be a model witch but a happy one who wishes to share what they have found since re-entering the craft. I have laid out my personal perceptions, opinions and experiences, so please feel free to agree or disagree with them, but most importantly, to find your own interpretations and your true path.

I sincerely hope that my teachings and methods of using Wicca for wellbeing can encourage you to find a way to start serving your happiness and letting go of perfection.

Blessed be, Harmony x

# Part 1
# Magick for the Mind

# 1.

# Intuition

Intuition sits at the forefront of everything that Wicca and witchcraft can teach us about ourselves. In witchcraft, we rely on our intuition to tell us what we want, what we need and what we should avoid (even if this is something that we have been yearning for). However, learning to trust your senses can be a long process, especially when you may have been depending on validation from others to guide you. Adding to the difficulty is that sometimes when you are truly living by your intuition, any manipulative and power-hungry people around you can feel threatened by this and become even more disrespecting of your boundaries.

When I was younger, I took the phrase in the Wiccan Rede 'If it harms none, do what you will' a bit too literally. The Wiccan Rede is a set of moral codes that Wiccans use to guide their lives (see Chapter 12), and I interpreted the phrase as meaning that everyone else could do pretty much what they wanted around me. This meant that I would avoid conflict at all costs, which unfortunately didn't help when it came to developing trust in myself. Constantly letting everyone walk over me meant that there was no room for my own thoughts and ideas, or to learn to have faith in my intuition.

Self-trust and acceptance are also the basis of self-love and healing, informing our choices in spellwork and an understanding of who we are and how we would like to express ourselves, spiritually. We all have the ability to be intuitive beings and to make healthier and happier choices for ourselves, but quite often we have to start by re-evaluating the way that we are making those choices. To begin to tap in to our intuition, we need to listen to it. I call this concept 'getting to know yourself'. This can generally be a tricky subject, as knowing yourself can imply that you have figured out your identity, that it is fixed and you are going to be sticking to it forever. But to me, knowing yourself means looking inside of yourself and creating a starting point from which to let genuine joy into your life. It's like opening a little door that helps you discover what actually sparks happiness within you, without any self-limiting or inflexible restrictions or narratives.

## A RITUAL FOR KNOWING YOURSELF

This first ritual is a small practice that signals to the universe our readiness to embody a more complete version of ourselves. Its purpose is to help you to start getting to know yourself without judgement, thereby kick-starting the re-emergence of your hidden intuition. I do this ritual once a year to check in with myself and make sure that I'm following a path that's right for me. So, if you already feel that you know what brings you joy, but want to give this a go, feel free! It's never a bad idea to do a personal check-in. Allow yourself the time you need to complete this ritual. It's really straightforward but a great way to start your intuitive journey!

**Intent:** Connecting with the different aspects of your inner self.

**Perfect time:** To be performed on a Sunday evening. Sundays are the day for spiritual change and healing spellwork.

**You will need:**

a bath or shower (*or even a wild swimming spot if you're feeling brave!*)
4 candles of your choice (*optional, but helps with the tone of the spell*)
meditation music (*optional*)
handful of rose petals to represent self-love (*petals from other favourite flowers can be used too*)
your Book of Shadows (*i.e. magickal journal*) and a pen

✳ Set aside a couple of hours out of your day. Give yourself a clear space in which to think, when you won't be distracted, and run yourself a bath or prepare to take a shower.

✳ Set your candles up in your bathroom to provide low lighting and place them at four points around the room, so that they surround you and create a space around you. Turn off any lights or draw the blinds for the full effect of the soft, relaxing candlelight. Put on some soothing meditation music if you wish and unwind.

**Bath method:**

✳ If you're in a bath, place your petals in the tub and make sure that the water is at a temperature that you can lie in for a while.

✳ If you wish to work with your journal prompts in the tub, begin by copying them down from the list below, on page 7, and then answering each one as casually as you want. Don't overthink the answers and ramble as much as you please; go with whatever comes to mind! (I started to journal in the bath, because I could be alone there with no interruptions. It feels like a safe space for me to be honest with myself, but if you would prefer not to write in the bath, continue with the journal prompts afterwards, in a place where you can relax and be undisturbed.)

⋆ After you have finished this task, have a full body wash. As you do this, try to visualise washing away your fears, self-criticisms, self-blaming and self-judgement. I like to visualise myself in a lake or stream, and that all of my past fears and self-given labels are rinsed away as the water flows around and past me. But don't worry if it feels as though your thoughts and emotions are still lingering. You are setting the intention of clearing the layers that are hiding your true self and walking away from them.

⋆ Be sure to blow out the candles at the end of the ritual.

**Shower method:**

⋆ Have a thorough and relaxing shower first (as with the bath method, you can visualise yourself washing away any fears and self-criticisms as you shower), then get out, dry yourself off, and complete the journal prompts below in a safe place.

⋆ If you are journaling after the shower or bath, and this leaves you too sleepy, go back to it the next morning, when you can be alone and able to focus.

⋆ Remember to keep safe by blowing out the candles after the ritual.

**Journal prompts:**

Journal prompts are simply ideas to get you thinking. Here are some that I find useful – but feel free to just use them as a starting point and to be creative with them and make up your own. Try not to only focus on regrets but look forwards, too! If you are struggling to find somewhere at home where you can concentrate, take yourself to a café or park to complete these journal prompts. I sometimes find it easier to concentrate in my favourite café when there is a lot going on or chaotic energy at home.

- When was the last time that you were truly happy and what was it that gave you joy at that time?
- Think of three things in your current or past life that make your heart sing.
- What is an activity or practice that truly makes you feel as though you have come home to yourself?
- What gives you a feeling of self-worth? (Is it from outside or internal validation?)
- When do you feel most beautiful, not to others, but to yourself?
- Which three moral values are especially important to you?
- How much do you value the opinions of others?
- Do you think that any of your life choices would be different had other people not influenced them?
- What is an interest, passion, hobby of yours, from your past or present, which reaches your soul?
- Would you do the job you have, wear the clothes you do and live the life you lead, if you could quickly start over?
- If you were capable of a fresh start, how would you go about it? (We can all make a fresh start, even if it feels out of our reach.)
- If you could imagine your ideal life in a year's time – how would you want it to be different to the present?
- What would your perfect day look like if there were no rules or expectations?

## PRACTICAL MAGICK TIP – SETTING YOUR INTENT

Intention lies at the heart of spellcraft. It's the energetic focus that we bring to magick when we think about the outcomes we wish to achieve. This is why it is so important to be clear about the intent behind your actions when you carry out rituals and spells, which means listening to yourself and trusting yourself.

# 2.

# Trust

The path towards learning to listen to yourself and trusting yourself, and developing faith in the world around you, can be life-changing. Sometimes, we can all feel like the odds are stacked against us, and whatever we are wishing for simply isn't working its way towards us. But Mother Nature is not against you and she never will be. She just *is*. She is a cycle of magick, creating life and holding your existence, every day.

We are neither above nor below nature; we just *are* nature. However, we can enhance our relationship with the earth by changing our thoughts and behaviour. Accepting what we can't change and changing what we can, is always a great starting point to work with. Are you regularly inviting negativity into your life, without a second thought? Are you repeating the same mistakes over and over again and expecting a different result? Do you treat yourself with disrespect and then attract people who do the same? It's important to be clear about what you want, so that the universe knows you are ready for your dreams. If you are permanently going against the mindset and life that you want to create for yourself, re-evaluation is needed!

To trust yourself fully, you have to grasp the concept that not everything is personal – the world does not have scales to measure if a person is good or bad; and it isn't against you – it's just life. You are neither a victim nor a hero, but a beautiful glimmer of light dancing in this universe for the short time that you have here. There will be beauty and there will be suffering, but every day we can learn from suffering and embrace beauty to make our time here as joyous as possible.

> PRACTICAL MAGICK TIP – BE PATIENT
>
> When things are becoming overwhelming, and your only choice is to wait and be patient, grab your journal, manifestation diary (a journal in which you make lists of the things you want to attract to your life) or Book of Shadows and write:
>
> *I trust the universe to give me what I need.*

# UNIVERSAL CYCLES

It is also beneficial to grow our connection with the world by putting our trust in cycles, such as the lunar cycle and the Wheel of the Year, which consists of the eight Sabbats or Wiccan festivals. By picking the right moments and acting accordingly, we can improve our manifestations and attract what we desire, therefore enriching our lives. When I started to trust the universe more, I began to have more faith in my body, spirit and capabilities. I started to understand that we are a part of this earth and we need to work with it and be more mindful of its natural phases.

## LUNAR CYCLES

Every month, there is a lunar or moon cycle, which you can make use of in your magickal practice. Rituals that need greater focus and the energy gained from the specific placement of the moon can be performed at relevant times. In addition, connecting with the earth's moon cycles can help you to enhance your intuition, to receive psychic messages, and generally help you to bond with the universe.

**The new moon** is amazing for any spellwork relating to new beginnings, transformation, and manifesting for the next moon cycle.

**The waxing moon** is a great time for inviting change, new growth and new arrivals, and for nurturing aspects of your career, or the blossoming of romance or friendships.

**The full moon** is a terrific time for any magick that needs a more significant lunar influence, especially relating to financial aspects of life, strength, power, change and psychic work.

**The waning moon** is a perfect time for anything that needs removing, breaking curses, moving on, cutting ties and banishing of any kind.

THE WHEEL OF THE YEAR

Some Wiccans like to follow the traditional pagan Wheel of the Year, which is an annual cycle of seasonal celebrations. There are various names and festivals for these days. For now, we will focus on the basics as we will be looking at them in more detail in Chapter 10; here are names of the key festivals in the Wheel of the Year and what each celebration represents.

**Samhain** takes place from 31 October to 1 November (in the Northern Hemisphere) or from 30 April to 1 May (in the Southern Hemisphere). The veil between us and the spiritual world lifts, and the Wheel of the Year has finished its cycle, allowing a new cycle to begin. We honour loss, the process of life, and give thanks.

**Yule** takes place on 20 to 24 December (in the Northern Hemisphere) or 20 to 23 June (in the Southern Hemisphere). We celebrate the shortest day and longest night, with themes such as thanking the year for an abundant harvest and welcoming the warmth that will arrive soon.

**Imbolc** takes place on 1 to 2 February (Northern Hemisphere) or 1 to 2 August (Southern Hemisphere). We celebrate the earth beginning to warm up, welcoming the forthcoming spring to the world.

**Ostara** (Spring Equinox) takes place on 19 to 22 March (Northern Hemisphere) or the 19 to 22 September (Southern Hemisphere). This is the celebration of the start of spring. Themes include the perfect balance of day and night, light taking over darkness, and preparation for the summer.

**Beltane** (May Day) is celebrated from 30 April to 1 May (Northern Hemisphere) or on 31 October to 1 November (Southern Hemisphere). Beltane is the peak of spring with themes of abundant growth, light, sexuality and fertility. It's a joyous celebration of warmth and thriving nature.

**Litha** (Summer Solstice) takes place on 20 to 24 June (Northern Hemisphere) or 20 to 24 December (Southern Hemisphere). We celebrate the longest day and shortest night of the year. Its significant themes are abundance, warmth, bountiful joy and remembering that there is still warmth to come.

**Lammas** (Lughnasadh) takes place on either 1 August (Northern Hemisphere) or the 1 February (Southern Hemisphere). It celebrates the harvest, the slowing down of growth, the rewards from the summer and recognising that we must soon start preparing for and welcoming the colder days.

**Mabon** (Autumn Equinox) takes place on 21 to 24 September (Northern Hemisphere) or 21 to 24 March (Southern Hemisphere). Mabon is a celebration of balance and gives thanks to the summer months for the things that we have received; it's a great time to let go, relinquish control and start to rest.

## WEEKDAYS

The days of the week have special energies that make them particularly suited for different types of magick.

**Monday** is a good day to perform any spellcraft associated with new beginnings, divination, divine feminine work, wisdom and travel.

**Tuesday** is the day of the week associated with action, conflict resolution, work, overcoming obstacles, cleansing and protection.

**Wednesday** is the day for communication spellwork as well as anything related to your job, finance, progression and creativity.

**Thursday** is the day for finding solutions, legal matters, inner strength, mental health, and physical health.

**Friday** is associated with love, sex, fertility, fun, excitement, relationships, birth, passion and welcoming something new into your life, whether this is a project, a friend or simply new energy.

**Saturday** is the day for spells involving family, manifestation, completion and letting go of anything that is holding you back.

**Sunday** is a perfect day for healing spells or rituals, creativity, peace, spiritual change and inner growth.

When working with the spells and rituals in this book, you might find it useful to consult this list so that you can enhance your spellcraft with the energy of the natural cycles.

## TRUST YOUR BODY'S CYCLES

The cycles of our bodies are of course also part of nature and the universe. In order to begin to have more trust in your body, start noting and recording its spiritual and biological cycles. The second part of this is easily applicable for people who menstruate. However, I believe everybody can benefit from noticing and reflecting on their bodies and their personal cycles throughout the month. See if you can spot patterns relating to your own body clock, such as moods, changes in how your body feels and fluctuating energy levels.

To begin to work with your menstruation cycle, start by documenting it every day, beginning with the first day of your bleed. Record your emotions and feelings, anything that you feel is relevant, and if you feel an intense urge to change anything. Do this every day until your next bleed.

Once you have done this, you can take the initiative to manifest specific things during your period. For example, on the first day, you can use any emotions that might have been building to set an intention for the rest of your cycle. You can also use this time to perform any magick that you feel needs extra focus or power behind it, such as the energies of fertility or releasing.

Another great way to learn to listen to yourself is through the art of meditation, which we'll be exploring next.

# 3.

# Life-changing Meditation

The word 'meditation' comes from the Latin *meditatum*, meaning 'to ponder'. At first, I thought that it had to be a lot more complex than this meaning suggests. I assumed that the goal was to silence my mind and master the art of not thinking. But in common with most apprentices of meditation, I came to realise that the practice teaches you to be in the position of an observer. Once I was able to let go of my expectations and pre-conceptions, I really began to benefit from its effects. Meditation is a great way to connect with your inner self, to develop trust in yourself and find calm.

The fast pace of daily life can hinder our happiness and meditation can be a solution to that. Starting to take part in a slow practice in which you allow yourself time to be and exist in the present, with no goals or agenda, no effort, just being, can really help you to achieve some balance in life. Meditating regularly has such amazing, life-changing effects and, after a while, it really does feel as though your soul catches up with you and allows you to come home to yourself.

When I first started meditating, I was practising maybe once or twice a week, usually to calm any anxiety that I had and sometimes for visualisations before spellwork. Then last year, I began to meditate every day and this regularity changed everything. I found that doing a simple ten to thirty minutes of meditation each day helps me to stay grounded and enables me to delve into getting to know parts of myself that I had previously kept hidden.

As well as being a fabulous grounding experience, it can also help attach your subconscious to your conscious self, enabling you to connect with your intuition on a greater level. And because meditation places you in the role of the onlooker, it can help you become more aware of the world around you and the part that you play within the universe.

Not everyone approaches the practice of meditation in the same way; some people simply choose to take long walks or sit in silence with a cup of tea for fifteen minutes a day. If you are interested in exploring further into how meditation can help you to get to know yourself, there are an unlimited number of focus-based practices to explore, that will help you to reach inside your subconscious mind. This approach helped me to connect further with deities, with my inner child (see Chapter 4) and also assisted me with divination. Here are some of the most effective and enlightening meditations that I've tried, along with short explanations of the purpose of each one.

## DAILY STARTER MEDITATION

This first meditation practice might seem a little introductory. Still, I feel that it's best to start at the basics if you are a beginner, before going deeper into what meditation can do for you. Approach this meditation with a beginner's mind, get ready to experience new emotions and feelings, and to just be here.

**Perfect time:** Find a place where you won't be disturbed for anywhere between 5 to 20 minutes. You can increase your meditation time a little day by day if you feel this works best for you.

Intent: To create a foundational meditation practice.

**You will need:**

a timer
soothing music (*optional*)

✶ Set a timer so that you're not focused on when you need to stop meditating. Put on some music before you start if you wish, or enjoy the silence. You can be seated or lying down.

✶ Close your eyes and take three full, deep breaths.

✶ Focus on where the air is entering your body, the tips of your nostrils or your mouth, and follow it, trying to keep a regular flow of breath.

✶ Allow thoughts to come, but avoid getting caught up in them. If you realise you have drifted away, keep coming back to your breath. This practice may feel difficult at the beginning, but don't punish yourself! It will get so much easier, the more times that you try it.

✶ At the end of your meditation time, gently allow yourself to return to everyday life. Don't go on your phone or instantly find a distraction. Sit with yourself for a while or slowly get on with a daily task and reflect on how the meditation practice made you feel.

## CONNECTING WITH YOUR DEITIES

This introductory meditation will help you to bond with any deities that you wish to, or that you are already working with. It allows you to open your mind to the gifts of gods and goddesses and whatever they represent to you, and any psychic messages that you might need to hear. For example, I was working with a deity last year and I had already created a vision of her in my imagination. While I was meditating, I suddenly

18

felt the overwhelming urge to do yoga, which felt like it was a message from this goddess to begin my yoga journey.

**Intent:** To connect to divinities and their messages for you.

★ Find a place to sit where you are comfortable. Close your eyes and, in your mind, envisage the deity that you wish to bond with, using any pictorial references or symbols that represent them. Or you can imagine how the deity feels to you or what this divinity means to you.

★ Once you have your deity or their essence in mind, feel free to ask them (mentally or verbally) if they have a message for you. After you've done this, retain the thought for a second, and see what comes into your head.

★ Document any thoughts or images that you might have, as this may hold a message, an idea, or an insight into your past, present or future.

★ After spending some time bonding with your divinities during this and other practices, you might be able to ask more specific questions while meditating.

## WHERE DO I GROW NEXT?

This meditation can be used to help receive psychic messages from the universe. It enables you to understand the next moves that you need to take in regards to inner growth. I created this meditation entirely by accident. While meditating, I imagined myself passing through a door and immediately thought, 'Massage!' which led me to start healing an unhealthy relationship with my body. I then continued to use this practice with great results.

**Intent:** To tune in to messages from the universe.

✴ Find yourself a comfortable seat, with your back supported and where you can be still for a few moments. Again, music is optional.

✴ Lower your gaze or, if you find it easier, close your eyes. Picture yourself at a door, open it slowly and pass through into darkness. When you are in the fertile darkness, think to yourself, 'What next?'

✴ Retain that thought for a few seconds, and whatever comes to mind will represent a pathway, a move or a message about what needs doing or looking into next.

✴ Please write it down and act on it as soon as possible!

## MANIFESTATION MEDITATION

This is a visualisation meditation, commonly used before spells to help increase the energy and the intentions of the spell. This practice will help you place your manifestations out into the universe and thereby attract what you desire into your life. Visualising your goals can help you start to turn them into your reality. If you visualise with focus, the universe and your subconscious will clearly recognise that this is what you're asking for yourself and the world around you!

**Intent:** To put your manifestations – your desires and wishes – out into the universe.

**Perfect time:** Perform this meditation in the evening before a new moon.

**You will need:**

your magickal journal or Book of Shadows
a pen

a crystal that you feel very connected to
1 coloured tea light candle (*use your intuition to choose the colour*)
box of matches or lighter
timer

⋆ Grab your journal or Book of Shadows and write down your manifestations for the duration of the next moon cycle, or anything you'd like to 'plant' or initiate this month. For example, if you want to change your job in the near future, you could write, 'The seed for my next job will be planted soon.'

⋆ After you've written your manifestations, place your chosen crystal on top of your book, leaving it open on the relevant page.

⋆ Light your tea light and place it near the book, on a plate for safety.

⋆ Place the book and candle in front of you.

⋆ Sit comfortably on a chair or on the floor, and set a timer for 5 minutes. Close your eyes and take some time to visualise your manifestations for the next moon cycle. Picture yourself already having acquired or received them. After you've finished, open your eyes and hold your hands up to the sky and say the words:

*I thank you for blessing me with these gifts.*

⋆ Blow out your candle and make sure that your book is placed on a windowsill or somewhere in full view of the moon, which may not yet be visible in the sky. The following day you can remove your crystal and your book.

✶ Over the next cycle, look out for opportunities heading your way and place your plans into action. Manifestations will never work if you don't want them enough!

## SUNRISE MEDITATION

This meditation creates focus first thing in the morning. This is my preferred regular practice as it can help me feel incredibly calm during my day. I've included two options to try. The first version is for beginners, while those with a little more experience might want to try the second.

**Intent:** To create a supportive and calming mindset for the day ahead.

**Perfect time:** If you ever get the chance, try this as the sun is rising! It's a beautiful experience. If you are feeling adventurous, you could even practise this meditation outside at sunrise.

**You will need:**

sunrise meditation music (*optional*)
a timer

✶ Start by preparing your area. Open your curtains or blinds, find yourself a comfortable place to sit, and put on some sunrise meditation music if you fancy it.

✶ Set a timer for 5 to 10 minutes.

✶ Sit with your legs crossed and place your hands on your knees with your palms facing upwards, with your thumb and your index finger together. This hand position is called the 'Gyan mudra'. It is used to help improve focus and keep your energy balanced throughout the practice.

✭ Take a few deep breaths, then close your eyes or lower your gaze.

**Option No. 1:**

- Take this time to focus on the breath entering your body. Every time you have a thought that you get caught up in, gently brush it away, then focus once again on your breath.

**Option No. 2:**

- Envision the sun and its glow, synchronise its glow with your breath until you feel ready to end your practice.

✭ After you've finished, take a few moments to sit and look outside, or around you if you are outdoors. Take note of the news that comes with every day.

## AFTERNOON MEDITATION

This meditation is best used as a short decompression as your day progresses. If you already practise meditation in the mornings, it might still be a great way to help you progress. Quite often, the period after lunch can be overwhelming, when you are at the peak of your day, tension is high, and your practice from the morning may be floating away from you. This could be particularly relevant if you have a stressful job or other ongoing pressures in your life.

**Intent:** To release a build-up of stress during the day.

Perfect time: This meditation can be performed in a quiet area at work or home anytime between midday to 4 p.m.

**You will need:**

a timer

★ Find a favourite spot and set a timer so that you can wind down for anything between 3 to 20 minutes. It's your choice whether to close your eyes or lower your gaze, depending on what is comfortable.

★ Place your left hand on your upper chest and your right hand above your belly button to begin. The chakras are the main energy centres of the body, and this hand position helps connect your heart chakra to your solar plexus chakra, creating balance within.

★ Take three deep breaths and then spend some time focusing your energy at the centre point between your hands.

★ As you breathe, focus into the space that you can feel in between your hands. If you lose focus, return to breathing into the space.

★ After you've finished this practice, place your hands together in a prayer position for a few moments.

## EVENING MEDITATION

Giving yourself some space to relax and catch up with yourself can really improve your sleep and lower your anxiety. It can also encourage peaceful dreaming – giving your mind an opportunity to process your thoughts and emotions.

**Intent:** To relax and encourage healing dreams.

Perfect time: This meditation is to be performed on your bed, before you turn in for the night. You can wear headphones and listen to calming music or sit in silence, depending on what you prefer.

**You will need:**

1 blue, black or dark purple candle (*optional – these colours can help encourage a peaceful night's sleep and aid in psychic healing*)
a timer

✴ Start this practice by lighting your choice of candle if using. Place it somewhere safe where it won't be disturbed.

✴ Set a timer for 5 minutes or fewer, as you want to avoid falling asleep during this practice.

✴ Now lie down on your bed, take a few deep breaths, and then close your eyes.

✴ Slowly and steadily count to 10, timing each in-breath with each number, then breathing out. If you lose focus, remember to let go of whatever you're thinking about. Then return to where you were in your counting or start again at 1.

✴ When you've finished, be sure to extinguish the candle and try not to spend any more time on your phone that evening and to get to bed soon after this practice.

## COLOUR MEDITATIONS – USING DIFFERENT COLOURS TO HEAL

Colours are powerful tools within spellwork and spiritual practice. They can work with the chakras and trigger different emotions. This is why focusing on a specific colour can be an exciting form of visualisation that can help you to create a specific intention. Colour can also help heal a particular area of your life if you visualise a sphere of a particular shade while you meditate. The rainbow of many shades and variations might work differently for each of us – and assist us all with different purposes.

## BLACK

Visualising black can be a little tricky as our minds, when blank, are a black space. I prefer to imagine a black glow or allow my mind to be empty for this practice. Visualise black for enhanced focus in spellwork, relaxation, and for manifesting endings and new beginnings. Black can also help you to connect to male-energy based deities.

## RED

Visualising red can help you connect to your sexuality and your divine feminine, enhance sexual energy and uncover passions. Red can also help you to increase your inner fire and drive when needed.

## ORANGE

Visualise orange during your meditations to awaken your creative self or clear creative blocks. Orange can also assist you in making choices or help push you to make important decisions, especially within work and business. Orange also deepens inner warmth and love.

## YELLOW

Yellow can help connection with your inner child (see Chapter 4, page 30), enhance joy, strengthen reiki practices, and connect with the sun or deities related to the sun. Yellow is also a neutralising colour, so it is the best colour for calming and releasing anger.

## PINK

Visualise pink to manifest romance, increase self-love, and help with any feelings of disconnection with your body. It can be a quick and easy way to restore inner peace when you are feeling overwhelmed or anxious.

## GREEN

Visualise green for manifesting luck or strengthening luck spells, connecting with nature, supporting your connection with the fae, and helping with emotional and spiritual grounding.

## BLUE

Visualising blue during meditation is excellent for self-healing, awakening self-growth, and connecting with your shadow self (see Chapter 4, page 34). Blue can also promote inner calm and patience.

## PURPLE OR INDIGO

Visualising purple or indigo is excellent for divination. Visualise the colour and retain this for a moment – and then the first thought that you have when you release your focus will express whatever needs to be changed, acted on or approached. Purple and indigo are also great for strengthening manifestations and connecting with the moon.

## SILVER

Silver visualisation can help you to manifest money, connect with the moon and also to heighten power during spellwork.

Silver also enables individuals to connect to the womb and can help with womb healing.

## GOLD

Visualise gold during meditation to support powerful spells and to trigger inner transformation.

## WHITE

Visualise white for enhanced clarity of situations, to restore balance, and to manifest clearer days ahead. White can also connect you to feminine-energy based deities.

# 4.

# Connect with Your Inner Child and Shadow Self

We saw in the last chapter how meditation can help us find calm in the chaos. If our lives fall into habits and routines, it can be easy to forget who we are and to fall into a pattern of existing, rather than living. We might rush around, going from work to a night out, pursuing hobbies and visiting friends; but when we have a second of stillness, everything can feel hollow. When I stopped, it felt as though my world was two-dimensional, made out of paper, without the depth that I had experienced as a child. As children, we are so full of magic, and as life gets busier, the magic can get lost.

Something that many of us lose as we grow up is the ability to be still. When we are preoccupied with our smartphones, forty-hour working weeks and weekends spent partying, the years can flash by, and we can't remember the last time that we were just being rather than doing. By rushing through life – always trying to get to the end of something – we seem to lose the spirit of it. So why the hurry? Why do we forget to pause and admire the sky, the birds and the flowers? When did we stop tasting our food and listening to the breeze in the trees? Do we want to lose these experiences forever, or do we want them back?

Yet it can also be very troubling to slow down, as when we

try to do this, we are often hit with a wave of emotions that can be mentally overwhelming. So be gentle with yourself and allow yourself dedicated time for a mindful walk, a five to ten-minute daily meditation, or the space to have a cup of tea in the mornings without any other distractions.

Practices within Wicca can also help us get to know ourselves further; divination, for example, is the perfect way to gain insight from within and receive psychic messages. During my healing journey, tarot reading helped massively to assist me in discovering parts of my subconscious that I thought that I had lost forever.

The essence of true self-love and wellness is finding our way back to our soul and re-learning how to live beautifully. A great way to start rediscovering who we are is through connecting with our inner child and our shadow selves. Though this is not a Wiccan concept but a therapeutic practice, I use meditation and divination to help me with these connections too.

## REDISCOVER YOUR INNER CHILD

Relating with our inner child can teach us patience, compassion and admiration for ourselves; feelings that might seem impossible at some points in our lives. By thinking about the inner child inside all of us, we can reflect on how we treat ourselves and others. For example, we would never let anyone harm a child, and we would want to encourage a child to be creative and express themselves. We would never tell them that they are ugly or worthless! So, what happens if we think of ourselves as a child – and remember that we are *still* that same young life, just grown up – and we still deserve the same care and kindness? Acknowledging and thinking about my younger self made me gentler with myself, helped me to find joy in the little things, and to gain a greater sense of presence – and hopefully it will be the same for you.

## INNER CHILD MEDITATION

Meeting your inner child is a beautiful experience. When I first did this meditation, a vision of my inner child sitting under a giant sycamore tree appeared. I instantly wanted to nurture this young being. It gave me a significant perspective on how I spoke to myself, how much I valued the childish joy of life, and how the little things seemed so precious to me when I was younger. My inner child is still within me – as yours is within you.

**Perfect time:** Find a spot that you feel safe in, whether outside in nature or in a room in your home. Either way, make sure you won't be disturbed for a while.

**You will need:**

a cushion or pillow
your magickal journal or Book of Shadows

✴ Cross your legs if you can, then take a cushion or pillow and place it in your lap with your hands on top of it.

✴ When you are settled, take three deep breaths, closing your eyes on the last breath.

✴ Once you've closed your eyes, visualise a tree. Sitting beneath the tree is you, as a child, with all of your misunderstandings, faults and flaws, but also all of your beauty and innocence.

✴ Picture yourself hugging the child and nurturing them. Do not leave the inner child; take your time and when you are ready, open your eyes.

✴ Afterwards, journal about your experience.

**Journal prompts:**

Here are a few questions to ask yourself if you would like some prompts. These are just suggestions – think about your younger self and follow your heart.

• How did it feel when you met your inner child?
• Can you think of ways that you mistreat yourself or relate to yourself now that you would never put that inner child through?
• What are some of the qualities that you value in your inner child? (For example, their freedom, innocence, interest in hobbies, willingness to try new things, curiosity.)
• Ask yourself: how can you get closer to your inner child? For example, could you re-parent them? Could you make

a conscious effort to unlearn taught patterns of behaviour and relearn a healthier approach? Or maybe you often feel as though you want to take inspiration from your childhood and be more hands-on and practical and use technology less?

## AN INNER CHILD TAROT SPREAD

Tarot reading helps us connect with our subconscious. This inner child tarot formation is a brilliant practice that you can use as a toe-dipping exercise to help you discover your young inner self again, build up self-trust and understand what inner child work can do for you.

**You will need:**

your favourite tarot deck
a journal or paper and pen

✴ Focus on connecting with your inner child while shuffling the deck. Pull your cards from the top or randomly from the deck – whatever feels right for you. You could place your hand over the cards until you are pulled towards the energy of the ones that you need. Then place 5 cards in a straight horizontal line.

✴ Take your time to consider each card and think about its qualities:

**Your first card represents**: something that you wanted but couldn't have as a child (material or otherwise).

**Your second card means**: what you should focus on to help you connect to your inner child.

**Your third card addresses the question**: is there something in your life that's holding you back from feeling joy?

—
33

**Your fourth card represents**: how you should act to stop this obstruction from holding you back.

**Your fifth card represents**: a message that your inner child wants you to hear.

✳ Be sure to journal the answers to this spread and bear them in mind as you work closely with your inner child. You may not understand the outcomes at first, but they might become more apparent through further tarot work and reflection.

## EMBRACING THE SHADOW SELF

Connecting with your shadow self is just as important as connecting with your inner child, although this might feel more daunting. The shadow self is the side that we *all* have but which we typically choose to hide, even from ourselves. It's the guilty, jealous, angry, resentful side that we often don't acknowledge and for whose faults we habitually place the blame elsewhere. Despite this, your shadow self isn't evil or corrupt and it needs to be understood, accepted, forgiven and worked with if you want to find inner peace.

Understanding what lies in our darker areas can help us work with our shadow selves and deal with unresolved, negative or uncomfortable emotions. Knowing yourself well enough to recognise when these emotions are triggered can help you to make changes, no longer allowing these feelings to control you. You cannot celebrate some of the lighter and fluffier parts of yourself if you're not willing to look at the darker ones.

Shadow work also helped me to uncover trauma that was affecting me negatively because I was hiding it and not dealing with it. Once you accept these sorts of challenging emotions, it's easier to find the route and move forward without letting them get in the way of your happiness.

# A SHADOW-SELF TAROT SPREAD

This tarot spread is a small step towards working with your shadow self; use your immediate intuition while reading these cards and listen to whatever thoughts and emotions come to the surface!

**You will need:**

your favourite tarot deck
a journal or paper and a pen

✶ Think about your shadow self while shuffling the deck. Then place 5 cards in a horizontal line.

**Your first card addresses the question**: where does my shadow self appear in my days or where has it appeared recently?

**Your second card answers the question**: what is my shadow self struggling with right now?

**Your third card addresses the question**: what action do I need to take to assist my shadow self?

**Your fourth card answers the question**: what is my shadow self trying to tell me needs healing?

**Your fifth card addresses the question**: am I self-sabotaging in any way right now?

✶ Once again, make sure that you have your journal handy to record the outcome from each question. You may not under-stand the outcomes at first, but they might become more apparent through further tarot work and reflection.

# YOUR WANTS ARE IMPORTANT

Shadow work and inner child work can both help you to realise the importance of recognising and working with your wants and desires. Constant longing is not good for us. We have to understand that sometimes we want something that isn't good for us and will never make us truly happy, but we are the only ones who can do something about this! So, we must choose carefully around what to focus on and what to let go of.

Once you get to know yourself, you may find that your wants change and shift. True desires are usually not fleeting – they are whole and grounded. Witchcraft can teach us to move with our wishes slowly and choose the right time to manifest these wants into reality.

Both shadow work and inner child work can help us to remove blocks and to acknowledge and express more of our true selves in the world – and one way to do this is through art magick.

# 5.

# Art Magick

Making art of any kind can be a means of healthy emotional expression while also building self-confidence and inner trust. As we bring our authentic selves to the world, communicating without barriers or limitations, we are opting to show our vulnerabilities – and that can feel extremely empowering. Combining our exposed emotions with intention, and then articulating this onto a canvas, paper or fabric, or with a musical instrument or whatever takes your fancy, can help you to shift your energy and release something that simply can't be kept inside you anymore.

Making authentic art from your personal experience is powerful in itself, so it's no wonder that creativity can be used within witchcraft. Art can be used as a tool for spellwork that is made particularly effective by the emotions, energy and time invested in it. So it makes sense that we can consciously place an intention into our creations for effective results too. What could be more magickal than putting a mood, memory, or emotion into a painting that will be displayed, helping to add or remove energy from a room?

Unfortunately, I spent a long time believing that the point of painting, drawing or doing any kind of making was the end product, forgetting that we are put on this earth for no specific reason, so joy should be at the top of our priority list. Yes, by all means set yourself small objectives if it motivates you to do something that you love, but creativity is not something that should be measured by its end result or whether the outcome might sell. Instead it should be used as an expression of emotions, thoughts, love and reflection.

We also sometimes need reminding that we can find immense pleasure in self-expression and creating art and music without feeling as though we have to be working towards doing something spectacular or life-changing. We can gain contentment from making things solely for personal pleasure and fulfilment, and just being in the moment. In my personal journey, painting was a replacement for releasing my feelings in less healthy habits. Sometimes I'd get to the end of my week, want to go out and have a few drinks, but instead, I stayed at home and painted, and it gave me a surprisingly similar feeling of release.

## SETTING THE TONE FOR MAGICKAL ART SESSIONS

Regardless of what your creative practice is, you can set up the environment to help your art magick produce effective results once you've imbued it with intention. For example, choosing relevant incense or coloured or scented candles to burn, crystals to leave on the finished product, and music to play can all be highly successful ways to invoke the emotional intent behind the piece if you wish. You can also time your artistic sessions to coincide with the moon phase or certain days of the week to enhance the purpose of your magickal artwork (see Chapter 2, pages 11–14).

### TOOLS TO USE

Within art magick, you can turn any primary tool that you use for your artistic practice into a 'wand' or director, to help concentrate energy into whatever you're making. Items such as knitting needles, paint brushes, crochet hooks, lino cutting tools and even guitar pics can be used as a point of energy focus. But, of course, your hands are excellent (and powerful) energy directors too. So, if using tools isn't your style or you don't feel the need to make any of your devices into a 'wand', your hands will do the job for you.

## CONSECRATING YOUR MAGICKAL TOOLS

To make a specific tool into an appropriate director of magickal energy, you will need to consecrate it. Doing this clears the item of any previous energy that it might be carrying. Consecrating it will also help the tool work alongside the four elements – these being the elemental powers of Earth, Air, Fire and Water, which correspond with the cardinal points of north, east, south and west – meaning that your tool will be blessed from every direction.

**Intent:** To purify your tools for magickal work.

**Perfect time:** The full moon is a good time to perform this ritual.

**You will need:**

salt
incense
candle
water

✶ First, you will need to represent the elements in the shape of a circle that surrounds you. To do this, put salt in a dish, set to the north of the circle, to represent the Earth. Light incense to represent Air and place this at the east. A lit candle positioned to the south of you will represent Fire, and a dish of water placed to the west of you will represent Water.

✳ Now face east and announce, 'I choose this (name of your tool) to assist me within my work.' Still facing east, pass the tool through the incense smoke, and say, 'Element of Air, I choose this tool (naming the tool again) to assist me in my work.'

✳ Move around the circle in a clockwise direction, and repeat the phrase for every element, adjusting the wording according to which element you are addressing. While doing this, quickly pass the wand through the lit flame or just above it when you are facing south, sprinkle water over the tool when you are facing west and finally sprinkle salt over the tool when you are looking north.

✳ Once you have completed consecrating your tool with every element, hold it above your head and say, 'This tool is ready to assist me within my work, being consecrated and charged, so blessed this (name of tool) be.'

✳ You can also decorate the tool with relevant symbols, such as the four elements or protection symbols, to support its energy.

## EXPRESS YOUR CREATIVE SELF

Every one of us is born with imaginative and inventive potential. We have an innate need to work with the earth, to build, design and express ourselves. When I woke up my creative side, a fire started inside me. It allowed me to have an outlet to express my emotions and give myself time to appreciate the beauty of life and how, as humans, we want to experience and capture that splendour through art and making. Use this ritual to give yourself that gift too.

# RITUAL TO AWAKEN YOUR CREATIVITY

As well as charging your tools with intention, you can perform a simple yet powerful ritual for awakening your creativity. During this spell, we will be focusing on painting your essence – your soul, and what it looks and feels like to you. What came to me in the course of this ritual, for example, was the curved shape of a figure or spirit, bursting with colour and with further radiance within it and surrounding it. I painted with oranges, reds and maroons. I also painted a little white light inside the figure, representing the brightness returning to my soul. In the same way, allow yourself to paint whatever comes to you, using whatever colours you are drawn to.

**Intent:** To awaken your creativity and connect with your soul.

**You will need:**

canvas, paper or any base that you would like to use
pencil
paint (*listen to your intuition when it comes to colours!*)
paintbrush or any painting tools that take your fancy

*Optional extras:*
incense (*vanilla or lemongrass might be good to try here*)
crystals such as malachite and aquamarine
moon water to dip your paintbrushes in (*see page 46 for how to make this*)

✴ Start by setting up your area. Try to make this a spiritual experience and a pleasant one too. Give yourself time, light a candle and/or incense, gather your favourite crystals nearby and have your blank canvas in front of you.

✴ Now draw the sigil below in pencil to activate the painting. (A sigil is a symbol that has magickal power, see below.)

---

The idea is to paint over the sigil. The energetic charge of this sigil roughly translates as 'allowing my creative light to flourish and welcoming the gifts that creativity brings into my life':

★ Once you have drawn your sigil, begin painting. Your painting could be anything you wish; use your intuition and stick with it. Don't place any judgement on whatever comes to the paper, and allow your hands to flow freely.

★ Once you have finished, display the painting somewhere until you feel you no longer need to see it. If you wish, you can recharge your painting with a crystal when you think you need to renew your creative energy.

★ For a few weeks after this ritual, you may feel the pull to do something creative in other fields, so allow your intuition to guide you to other forms of expression! Enjoy just trying things out – with no expectations.

## INCORPORATING INTENTION INTO ART WITH SIGILS

Sigil comes from the Latin *sigillum*, meaning 'seal'. They are a popular form of magick, commonly made up by taking a word, letter or number and simplifying it to make a symbol. Sigils take our subconscious thoughts, intentions or desires and place them into a shape that helps turn aims into reality. It's a simple way of letting the world know what we want or need and helps enhance spellwork.

Drawing something with purpose and intention connects our subconscious mind to the physical world. As with any art form, this act channels our subconscious mind directly into reality, pushing through any internal blocks that we construct as conscious humans, thereby serving the purpose and the result of a spell.

## HOW TO CREATE A SIGIL OF YOUR OWN

It is simple to make your own sigils to use in rituals and spell-craft once you are clear about the sort of magickal activation that you'd like to achieve.

**You will need:**

pen and paper

* Start by taking a word or phrase that represents the type of magickal activation you'd like to achieve. For example, suppose I was doing a banishing activation to let go of a past relationship; in that case, I could take the phrase 'I release this relationship.' Or, if I was adding a sigil to a ritual I was doing, I may take a simple word prompt like 'joy,' 'rest,' or 'banish.'

* Begin by writing down your phrase or word in full.

* Now take your phrase and remove any repeated letters from it. For this example, I will be using the phrase 'I am at peace and I am loved.' Therefore, once I had removed all the doubled-up letters, I would be left with: T P C N L O V

* You can then remove the vowels; in this case, I would be left with: T P C N L V

✮ Now you can create a sigil with the letters as they are:

✮ Or you can go further and simplify the letters like this:

ll C ∧ Lov

✮ Then combine them in whatever creative way you wish to – here's my example:

✮ The final step you can include is placing the intention you have from the spell to the sigil. You can usually break this down into four categories:

• invoking (welcoming or bringing in)
• evoking (banishing or pushing out)
• manifesting (attracting)
• honouring (thanking and loving)

Depending on which category your spell falls within, incorporate a corresponding sigil.

• For an invoking spell, you could draw a circle around the sigil or incorporate it into the sigil:

• For an evoking spell, you could draw two lines crossing each other through the sigil:

- For a manifesting ritual, you could draw a line above and below the sigil:

- For an honouring ritual, you could draw a line either side of the sigil:

✴ If you are using a sigil for artwork, the emotion that you put into it generates the activation. If you are looking to activate sigils generally, you can meditate on them. To do this, visualise the sigil that you have created and its intention for a few minutes.

✴ You can also activate it by placing a relevant crystal on top of the sigil overnight, either outside or on a window facing the moon (the full or new moon is best!) Then remove the crystal in the morning. Another method is to sprinkle charged moon water onto the sigil while visualising the intention.

## BRINGING THE EARTH TO THE CANVAS

Another way to place an intention into your art is by working with nature and the magickal properties of particular herbs. The same goes for trees, leaves or mushrooms, etc. I could go on! As well as incorporating images of specific plants that reflect your meaning into your creations, you can also actually use the natural objects as a part of your artwork. You could create dyes and pigments using fruits, vegetables, tree resin or dirt to add a new layer of creativity. If you're into printing, you can make some fabulous marks, patterns and shapes from collected leaves, fruits, vegetables or seed cases.

## FURTHER IDEAS FOR CREATIVITY WITHIN WICCA

There are many other ways that you can combine magick with art and creativity. Here are a few to get you started:

- Making decorations for the Sabbats or Wiccan holidays – the key festivals in the Wheel of the Year (see Chapter 10)
- Knitting or crocheting a blanket with magickal words and symbols such as sigils
- Decorating a box with found natural objects such as shells
- Making, adapting and decorating clothes to wear for spellwork
- Creating collages and taking photos for use with your intentions and manifestations
- Origami
- Cooking

Enjoy experimenting and using creativity as a way to express your inner self in the outer world, giving your ideas and intentions a physical presence – which takes us to Part 2: Magick for the Body.

# Part 2
# Magick for the Body

# 6.

# Food and Cooking Magick

Along the course of my Wiccan path, I have variously tried to identify as a green Wiccan, eclectic Wiccan and a cottage Wiccan, and so forth. These labels resulted in me trying to restrict myself from practising certain types of magick that didn't seem to fit into a perceived particular classification. One of the beautiful things that happened when I allowed myself to flourish in a genuine way was that I discovered I could be spontaneous with whatever form of magick feels right for me at any time! One of the favourite areas that I love exploring is food and cooking magick. I am always surprised and inspired by the possibilities within kitchen witchery. And the thing that is most wonderful about this form of witchcraft is that because we are consuming whatever we are creating, its effects have double the strength.

I think we often overlook the relationship between what we are putting into our bodies and our sense of wellness. I don't think that the discussion around food has to be scary; enjoyable and mindful eating that works for us can bring so much pleasure to our lives! Within traditional Wiccan practices, using nourishment as a form of celebration is encouraged. Food is another connection that leads back to the earth, which is why I think putting emphasis and time into what you're eating is a crucial part of spiritual wellbeing. Food and drink can create magick of many kinds, as well as being a way to give thanks to the Sabbats and to offer to deities. The fact that we have the blessing of eating every day is magick within itself. The food that we eat has been grown and cared for and has a story to it. It fuels us and creates life within us, so being aware of the magick associated with food can raise our vibrations and promote grounding.

## MINDFUL CONSUMPTION

When it comes to kitchen witchery, there seems to be a variety of different approaches, but the awareness of what you're eating is crucial. I'm not saying that you should completely avoid fast food, or that we all need to be vegan or that everything we eat has to be organic. I just recommend encouraging mindfulness around where our food is sourced from and how we can help with creating better conditions for animals and fair wages for those that grow what ends up on our plates.

If we have access to locally grown food, opting for this can be helpful to our community and also a more mindful way of shopping. In addition, growing our own herbs, fruit and vegetables helps us to connect with the earth and enhances the energy behind any intention that we place on our food. And if we're choosing to eat meat and dairy, we can educate ourselves about the environmental effects of these choices and we can honour them. We could choose to give back to the earth by supporting charities, or by making a commitment to cut down on our meat and dairy intake. Vegetarians and vegans can also reflect on how to repay nature. If we're opting for genetically modified food, we could try consuming it consciously or creating meat replacements of our own.

There is a traditional belief in Wicca called the 'Law of Three', or 'Threefold Law', which states that everything we put out into the world, or take from the world, is returned to us three times over. For an example, I am a huge coffee lover, but the majority of coffee isn't ethically sourced and some people who work on coffee farms are horrendously underpaid and work in poor conditions. As I have the resources to buy smaller batch coffees that support farmers with fair pay, I do so. Basically, whatever you can manage is helpful. Your good intentions will always be worthwhile, no matter how big or small your actions are. We can accept that cruelty-free consumption is rarely attainable, but we can also choose to do our part and give recompense where we can.

## BE THERE WITH YOUR FOOD

When you eat or drink, try consuming whatever it is without distractions. Try not to watch YouTube or read a book at mealtimes. Instead, appreciate your food for the miraculous joy that it is. Allow your soul to join you for the ride and marvel in every bite or sip. This approach can be especially useful if you're placing magickal intention in a meal or beverage.

Starting with the complete basics, the enjoyment of drinking a hot beverage is a ritual within itself. The consumption of tea and coffee is a custom that most of us enjoy every day, mostly without thought. When my time is too limited to meditate, sitting down with a warm drink and observing the world is almost as effective for my peace of mind. Coffee and tea also have magickal properties that can be useful for many different rituals, spells, divination and they can be used to help set small, quick intentions throughout the day.

If we eat and drink mindfully, we are less likely to overindulge and will find it easier to take a temperate attitude to what we consume.

# THE MAGICK OF TEA

Different types of tea can be used to help boost a daily objective, for manifestation or to set the tone of a minor kitchen magick spell. Many teas are made from herbs, all carrying unique magickal properties; consuming these can help to manifest your purpose quickly and effectively.

If you wish to start the day by solidifying an intention, try drinking a particular tea related to that purpose:

**English breakfast tea** is a drink for focus, visualisation, action, change, transformation and resolution.

**Chamomile** is excellent for headaches, calming, inner peace, visualisation, night-time manifestation and emotional healing.

**Green tea** is wonderful for energy work, cleansing, new beginnings, career advances, creation, and abundance.

**Black tea** is great for use in divination or tea-leaf reading, protection, prosperity, travel manifestation and connecting with the moon.

**Nettle tea** is excellent for receiving psychic messages, inner growth, healing, connecting with the fae and the earth.

**Peppermint tea** can be used for cleansing, repelling negativity, banishing spells, luck, and emotional cleansing.

**Lemon balm tea** is great for astral travel, inner cleansing, connecting with your third eye and creativity.

**Rose or floral** tea is perfect for romance, love, self-love, self-healing, finding new relationships and starting new projects.

## THE MAGICK OF COFFEE

Coffee can be used in a similar way to tea, although it has some specific magickal properties of its own. Coffee can be consumed explicitly for cleansing, improving vitality, inner healing, energy spells and setting work- or career-related intentions. Its energy-giving properties can be a beautiful way to set a productive purpose. You can use the format above to form an intention with coffee for your day! You could add different seasonings, such as vanilla to attract love, vigour and intellectual strength to your day.

## SCRYING WITH COFFEE AND TEA

The art of reading tea leaves or coffee grounds is a complex form of divination. As with all divination, it can be used to seek insight into the present, past and future, and for spiritual guidance. This can easily fit into your day as a part of your morning coffee or tea ritual.

**You will need:**

loose leaf tea or freshly ground coffee
tea or coffee pot
your favourite light-coloured mug

✶ First, brew your tea or coffee, allowing coffee grounds or tea leaves to fall into your cup while pouring. If you don't stir your drink, the grounds or leaves will mostly sit at the bottom. *Tip:* don't add any milk!

✶ Sit consciously with your beverage and clear your mind. If you have any questions that you'd like to put forward, vocalise them or focus on them now and then keep them in mind throughout your drink. If you'd just like a general reading, keep a clear, open mind and heart.

✶ Once you have finished your drink, make sure that the liquid is gone. Take a look at the bottom of the mug, and you will see the remains of your beverage. Keep this still, and see what you can work out from the shapes formed by the leaves.

✶ Now is the time to use your intuition! You may be able to see animals, shapes, symbols, faces, etc., in your cup.

**A few rules I like to follow:**

• Don't overthink when you are working out what it is that you can see. Go with what stands out to you first; if you have to look too deeply, it might not be the right time for you to be trying this. You may only see one or two things in your cup, and that's perfectly okay.

• Please don't go on the internet and search for whatever image you find in your cup and the symbolism behind it – use your intuition first! If you can see a dragon, what does that mean to you? Fear? Freedom? Strength? What does it tell you about your current situation? Only

Google something if you are really struggling with working out what it could mean.
- Record what you see and how you interpret it; this might help you throughout the days and weeks to come.

★ After you've finished, recycle the grounds or leaves by returning them and their nutrients to the earth and wash your cup out.


## SOBRIETY

Earlier in this book, I touched on the subject of partying weekends, so I thought I would mention sobriety within Wicca. Traditionally, wine is used in rituals or sometimes as an offering, or as a symbolic beverage for celebrations. I believe that everything in moderation, approached from a mindful perspective, is a wise path. So, I'm not telling everyone to be sober, but I recommend maybe challenging or testing yourself over your intake. I also think that it is natural to have coping mechanisms, and it is very easy to fall into unhealthy ones.

During my journey to sobriety, I tried to find other ways to help me cope with times of trouble, such as reading, yoga, exercise and gaming. Meditating regularly also helped me to manage daily issues, because it kept me connected to my emotions and my thoughts.

If you feel there is anything that you rely on a little too much to keep you going, and this pattern of behaviour doesn't always result in you feeling your best, try taking a month or longer off from your coping mechanism to see how it helps you get to know yourself. This approach made me realise that I often had little confidence in social situations when I hadn't had an alcoholic drink, and I often ignored or buried essential lessons that I could have learnt from because they were difficult to handle. Sobriety also enabled me to improve my relationship with my conscious body, witchcraft and the earth, as alcohol always built a barrier of disconnection between myself and the universe, unfortunately, numbing both the good and the bad.

## SETTING THE TONE FOR KITCHEN WITCHERY

As well as making the beauty of the preparation and consumption of food a daily wellbeing ritual, setting the tone within your cooking space can be a wonderful way to enhance the intentions behind your kitchen witchery. If you don't want to explicitly place a purpose into your cooking, you can create a ritual through the simple practice of preparing something that fuels and nourishes your body. Creating something that you consume will fill your body with energy – and that is magick in itself. So, it only makes sense for mealtimes to be a grounding, ritualistic experience.

Suppose that you would like to set a more precise intention for a cooking spell? In that case, you can use a particular incense, coloured candles, verbal affirmations, specific tools and relevant herbs and ingredients in your spells that will reflect your aims, enhance your focus and direct your energy into the universe. For example, in much the same way that you can consecrate tools for making art, some witches engrave symbols into a spoon or utensil to bless it. This item then becomes a type of kitchen witchery spoon or wand that can be used to help direct energy into whatever is cooking.

## HERBAL ADDITIONS TO YOUR MEALS

Herbs, seasonings and basically all other ingredients are a perfect way to set the tone for your spells. Some have quick and scientifically proven effects (if you're a witch who works best with facts!). Seasoning and herbs that you may already use in your food have magickal properties that add to your mealtimes. Take basil, for an example; it has impressive, positive properties! Whichever ingredient you choose, you can relate it to a specific intention that you'd like to set with your meal; it could be to uplift, to calm, to energise, or to bring extra passion to a relationship. Of course, you don't have to incorporate magick into every recipe, but I like to spontaneously include whatever I feel that I need at that particular mealtime.

Here is a list of well-known edible ingredients to add to your cooking as a part of your spellwork.

## SWEET

**Apple:** healing, love, strengthening psychic messages.

**Bananas:** inner and physical strength, sexual stamina, luck and vitality.

**Blackberries:** home protection and manifestation.

**Chocolate:** intimate relationships, fertility, love, self-love, inner strength and calm.

**Cinnamon:** calm, mental strength, luck and passion.

**Elderberries:** protection and purification.

**Ginger:** self-assurance, sensuality and calm.

**Mint:** energy giver, emotional and physical soothing, clears emotional blockages and helps the digestive system.

**Oranges:** creativity, inner warmth, cleansing, protecting and an anti-depressant.

**Strawberries:** luck, inner-love, calm, peace and healing.

**Sugar:** love, self-love, mood improvement and healing from heartbreak.

**Walnuts:** concentration, focus, understanding and creativity.

# SAVOURY

**Avocado:** male vitality, strength, fertility and stability.
**Basil:** good fortune, love and joy.
**Bay:** cleansing and protecting from negative power.
**Cayenne:** protection, healing from physical pain and
spiritual cleansing.
**Cumin:** protection, helps attract friendship and loyalty.
**Carrots:** psychic connections, female fertility, inner strength
and lust.
**Courgette:** stamina, work, encouraging vigour and
productivity.
**Dill:** protection, luck and a yoni activation herb.
**Fennel:** sexuality, strength and menstrual soothing.
**Garlic:** emotional and physical clearing, uplifting energy and
physical strength.
**Onion:** emotional clearing, home protection, luck and
manifesting.
**Potatoes:** comfort, stability, inner calm and healing.
**Parsley:** passion, divination, fertility and help in
receiving psychic messages.
**Pepper:** banishing, emotional clearing, assists in bravery and
cleansing.
**Rosemary:** clarity, cleansing, breaking spells, healing and
mindfulness.
**Salt:** cleansing, cleaning, emotional clearing, emotional
protection and banishing.
**Tomatoes:** cleansing, dismissing energy and encouraging a
relaxed mind.
**Thyme:** purifying, inner calm, calming a room and cleansing.
**Turmeric:** digestion, passion, romance and fertility.

# A PEEK INTO A WICCAN'S COOKBOOK

Before I begin to practise kitchen magick, I like to create a small sign or art piece that features a kitchen blessing. This is a form of word magick that can be used before casting a spell in the area. I like to say my kitchen chant out loud before performing any magick there. Blessing your kitchen isn't necessary, although it can be an excellent alternative to casting a circle and is the perfect solution if you feel that you need a little extra protection.

I recommend starting by creating a little script of the kitchen chant, followed by some paintings or any decoration that you think would be appropriate to the blessing.

After you have allowed your blessing script to dry, charge your piece of art overnight by placing an intuitively picked crystal on it. (The full moon is the best time to do this!)

You could frame your script and hang it in your kitchen, or prop it up somewhere safe. Re-charge your artwork with your crystal when you need to.

Before you begin a spell in your kitchen, you may also want to start with a cleanse of some kind, then announce the chant three times over to activate it.

You can create your own chant, invoking a protective blessing, describing how the universe can assist you with your spellwork in this space and the magick that you will be working with. It doesn't have to rhyme, although some people prefer this as it creates a hypnotic quality that allows you to focus your intention.

Alternatively, you can use mine:

> *With this chant, I bless this kitchen*
> *with joy, peace, magick and healing.*
> *I call the elements to assist thee,*

*with the intention that I'm seeking.*
*Water from rain, river and sea,*
*bless my food and douse earth tree.*
*Fire from elements connecting,*
*allow this to activate my spell's energy.*
*Grains and green from the earth herself*
*allow me to nourish, grow and share.*
*Allow the smoke, steam and scents*
*to circle the room and cleanse the air.*
*Protect this spell while it assists me*
*from now and always to be,*
*So mote it be.*

## MAGICK LEMON CAKE

This is an older spell of mine and still a personal favourite as it involves cooking, magick and cake! This spell has been designed to create a calming aroma around the house, as well as using lemon and poppy seeds to cleanse the home and lift any negative energy that resides there. This cake can also be eaten for a restful pause in your day when needed.

**Intent:** Calming, cleansing, energetically balancing and relaxing.

**Perfect time:** Best baked during the waning moon, or on a Tuesday for added cleansing and protection.

**You will need:**

6 tbsp vegetable oil
280g (10oz) self-raising flour
200g (7oz) caster sugar
1 tsp baking powder
2 lemons (1 for baking, 1 for topping)

approx. 2 handfuls of poppy seeds
180ml (6fl oz) water
icing sugar for topping

*Optional extras:*
kitchen witchery spoon
cleansing incense

✶ Pre-heat your oven to 200°C (400°F).

✶ Start by setting the tone for the spell by lighting some incense if you wish and gathering your ingredients so that you don't have to be rummaging around and interrupting your energy.

✶ Pour a small amount of oil in the bottom of your cake tin then line it with some baking parchment.

✶ Put your flour, sugar and baking powder into a bowl.

✶ Add the poppy seeds to the dry ingredients then while mixing say the words:

> *Allow these poppy seeds to calm my home,*
> *combine with these grains to bring me peace,*
> *relieve my exhaustion and*
> *balance this space's energy again.*

✶ Then add your water, the juice from your first lemon and the vegetable oil to the dry ingredients. While you are mixing in your wet ingredients, say the words:

> *Allow these ingredients to bond together,*
> *creating peace and cleansing this sacred area.*
> *Banish the negative, bring forward the positive,*
> *healing this place, so mote it be.*

✶ Your mixture should run off the spoon, so if it seems too thick, add a little extra water.

* Add your mixture to your lined tin and then place in the pre-heated oven for 25 to 35 minutes. Be sure to check the cake throughout the process to make sure that it doesn't burn!

* Open the interior doors in your home and close the windows to make sure the spell can work to its full effect! Feel any heaviness in your environment lift as the cake bakes.

* To prepare the icing, mix your icing sugar with the juice of the other lemon. The icing should be thickish, so use the amount of icing sugar that suits your preference!

* After the cake is done, allow to cool completely before adding the icing. Serve and enjoy for up to three days after baking for a relaxing treat when needed!

## SUNNY MARMALADE JAM SPELL

I often gravitate towards kitchen witchery by, for example, making jams, cakes and delicious treats that feel healing even without setting a magickal intention. I haven't always been a massive fan of marmalade, and I couldn't understand why you would ever want to eat fruit peelings on toast, let alone orange peel. However, I had a craving for it last year and decided to make a ritual. So I found some organic oranges, fresh lemon, added some ginger for its excellent healing properties, and went to town with it. It was delicious and brought me joy in every bite!

This spell intends to increase inner joy and allow it to radiate throughout your day. Oranges have cleansing properties, and ginger adds the benefits of pleasure and healing. The gold string helps represent joy and peace and keeps the magick contained until you can use the marmalade. This is the perfect spell to share with your loved ones as it makes quite a hearty amount of marmalade. I encourage you to put your inner love into this for the best results!

**Intent:** To increase your inner joy and love with every bite.

**Perfect time:** Sundays are best for added peace and love.

**You will need:**

1kg (2lb) oranges
2l (4pts) boiling water
1 whole lemon
1 heaped tbsp chopped ginger (*I recommend the stuff in the jar, but fresh is fine*)
1.5kg (3lb) granulated sugar
1 tbsp pectin (*optional*)

*Optional extras*:
kitchen witchery spoon
cheesecloth
sticky labels and pen
gold ribbon or string
sunstone crystal

✴ Before you begin cooking, make sure you have sterilised about 8 jars in the dishwasher or washed them thoroughly. Then rinse them with extra hot water and allow them to dry somewhere clean.

✴ Cut your oranges in half and squeeze the juice into a large saucepan. Remove any pips, pith and leftover pulp and place them to one side.

✴ Cut the orange peel into fine strips. Add these to the sauce-pan with the orange juice, the juiced lemon, chopped ginger and boiling water.

✶ *Optional*: you can, at this point, take your pips, pith and pulp mixture and place it in a cheesecloth, bundle it up into a ball and secure it. If you put this into the boiling water, attaching it to the handle of the pan, it will work as a binder to help the marmalade set. If you wish to use pectin instead, you can skip this step, and add the pectin after the next step.

✶ Simmer this mixture for two hours. *Optional*: after this time, remove the cheesecloth bag if using, allow it to cool and squeeze it so that the natural pectin is released back into the mixture.

✶ Now add the sugar to your pan and the pectin if using, bringing it to a low heat. Stir regularly in a clockwise direction with your kitchen witchery spoon to solidify the spell until the sugar has dissolved.

✶ To test your marmalade, add a small amount to a plate and leave it for a few minutes to check its consistency. If necessary, keep cooking until you are happy with the thickness, then leave the marmalade to cool in the pan.

✶ Take a sticky label and draw this sigil, which roughly translates as 'Abundant Joy':

Make one of these for each jar you will be using.

✶ Spoon the cooled marmalade into the sterilised jars. Stick on the intention labels and put the crystal by the jars to charge them. Tie the gold ribbon around each jar to preserve the magick and only untie when opening a fresh pot.

## LUCKY CINNAMON NEW MOON COOKIES

These vegan cinnamon cookies will provide you with an extra bit of good fortune for the new moon. New moons can either feel uplifting or draining, so depending on where I am emotionally and which moon it is (new moons are always a spiritually transformative time – regardless of whether you connect to them or not), I like to create something simple to welcome the moon and provide luck for myself and the new cycle to come. Overall, baked goods are simply wonderful for comfort, whatever the mood or tone that you're feeling from the new moon!

I sometimes cut out a small circle of paper, place it in the centre of the cookie and dust it with icing sugar, as this creates an empty space representing the phase of the moon.

As for the magickal properties of these cookies, cinnamon is fantastic for stability, luck and protection, whereas nutmeg provides luck and overall health. The dairy-free margarine can represent the earthly grounding element; flour contributes prosperity and rebirth, and sugar is terrific for banishing negativity. Finally, salt provides cleansing, while vanilla offers comfort and soothing for this next moon phase!

**Intent:** Providing luck for the next moon phase.

**Perfect time:** Any day during the new moon phase.

**You will need:**

250g (9oz) dairy-free margarine
220g (8oz) golden caster sugar
1 tbsp golden syrup

2 tsp vanilla extract
300g (11oz) plain flour
1 tsp baking powder
1 tsp cinnamon
1 tsp ground nutmeg
pinch of salt
icing sugar for dusting

*Optional extras:*
kitchen witchery spoon
paper and scissors (*to create template*)

* Preheat your oven to 180°C (350°F) and line a baking tray with parchment paper.

* Start by mixing the margarine, sugar, syrup and vanilla in a bowl until it forms a whipped cream-like consistency.

* When the mixture is thoroughly combined, add the flour, baking powder, cinnamon, nutmeg and salt, then combine completely.

* Roll the dough into small spheres around the size of a ping pong ball, and place them on the tray with enough space between them to allow the cookies to expand.

* Leave to cook for around 10 to 12 minutes, until the edges of each cookie are a golden colour.

* When finished, the cookies may still appear a little gooey in the middle but will harden as they cool.

* When cooled completely, place your paper template onto each cookie and dust with icing sugar.

* Enjoy these cookies for yourself and gift them to family and friends who may need some extra luck and love for this next moon phase!

# FLOWER-POWER SALAD FOR HEALTH AND PROSPERITY

The most important part of the spell, as we know, is the intention, and with this flower-power salad, it's essential to understand why you're creating it before preparing and enjoying it. Spells don't always have to include a magickal physical element. My great-grandmother Hilda used to say she could cast spells just from simply thinking about something, so with this particular spell it's all about the intention and the properties of the ingredients. This salad is a super way to welcome health and prosperity and can be prepared and made any time that the edible flowers are in season. It's a side-salad and can be enjoyed with an additional protein, such as delicious pine-nuts, or as a snack.

First, you will need to source edible flowers as not all flowers are safe to eat. The ones I suggest taste amazing, but if these aren't available, or you'd like to use your own flowers, research them thoroughly and wash them well before using them. And remember, as with all gifts from the natural world, consume everything in moderation.

Daises are remarkable for abundance and welcoming positivity, and pansies are well known for their aid in love spells and prosperity. For the base of the salad, we have rocket; a unique healer for the physical body and a curse repellent. We top this flavoursome salad with a dressing that includes salt, citrus and pepper, which are excellent for cleansing and deterring negativity. And this dish looks fabulous!

**Intent:** To welcome prosperity and good health to your mind and body.

**Perfect Time:** Springtime.

**You will need:**

1 handful of lettuce leaves of choice
1 handful of rocket
1 handful of fresh daisies
1 handful of fresh pansies
1 handful of marigolds
half a sweet onion
2 tbsp olive oil
a pinch of salt
ground pepper
lemon juice
1 tsp maple or agave syrup (*optional*)

☆ Start by washing your lettuce leaves and rocket and preparing a portion onto a plate or bowl. You can be the judge of how much greenery you'd like!

☆ Then cut your onion up into fine slices and place it on your lettuce bed.

☆ Follow this by removing any stalks from your flowers, washing them thoroughly, and patting them dry with kitchen paper. Then place them on top of your salad.

☆ Mix the olive oil, salt, pepper and lemon juice to taste in a bowl. Add a teaspoon of maple or agave syrup if you want something sweeter.

☆ Stir until combined, and then add to your salad, mixing the dressing into the leaves.

☆ Enjoy anytime you feel your body needs a pick-me-up!

## POST FULL MOON ORANGE COCOA

A full moon can be an emotionally transformative and heavy time, especially for women. The night after a full moon, you might feel drained of energy and ready for the new moon phase to begin. So why not nourish yourself with a cup of orange cocoa to allow the universe to let you know that you're ready to commit to yourself and re-charge.

Cocoa powder is a beautiful alternative to hot chocolate powder, as it typically has no added sugar and can be sweetened to taste. Not only that, cocoa has magickal properties, including welcoming comfort, contentment, and self-love. I combine this with orange, an excellent magickal cleanser, and sugar for re-charging the spirit, to create the perfect post full moon drink. Oat milk is also a fabulous grounding ingredient after the full moon, so I suggest using this, but many kinds of milk will have positive effects that you can benefit from.

**Intent:** To recharge after the full moon.

**Perfect time:** The morning after the full moon.

**You will need:**

1 cup of plant-based milk (*I recommend oat milk*)
1–2 tbsp cocoa powder (*to taste*)
sugar to taste
½ tsp orange essence

*Optional extras:*
small kitchen witchery spoon
a splash of single vegan cream (*why not make it extra special!*)
little vegan marshmallows

✶ Start by putting your milk, cocoa powder and sugar into a pan, and warm at medium heat until it's hot.

✶ Add the orange essence, and a splash of single vegan cream (if using) before whisking in and pouring into your mug.

* Take your small spoon and stir three times in a clockwise direction. As you do this, recite these words:

> *The moon shines bright,*
> *in all the joy and all the light.*
> *Allow me to re-charge and recollect*
> *before the next moon and I connect.*

* Now add your vegan marshmallows and a little extra cocoa powder and sugar dusting on top if you wish.

* Enjoy and spend some time relaxing as you sip your beverage.

Of course, life is all about balance and harmony. Whenever possible, magickal food and drink should be part of a healthy lifestyle that ideally includes an element of physical activity of some kind. Our bodies can be channels for magick too, as we will see next.

# 7.

# Magickal Movement

Physical movement can be a profoundly spiritual experience. Back in my teens, when I started running, it was the first time that I made the connection between being outside, feeling the fresh air in my lungs, and aligning my body and mind. I have also come to understand and appreciate the mindful elements of hiking, running, yoga and dancing. All of these methods of movement can be expressive and can connect you to your surroundings, which in turn, helps you to liberate yourself.

There is something very primal and human about pushing our bodies or minds into doing something that will help us in the long term. I don't know if that is because exercise directly links back to ancient survival or because of the endorphins that are released. Still, I know it's something that I feel myself wanting to do more and more as I get further into my spiritual journey. (I also want to mention that this perspective comes from someone with no disabilities or chronic pain and who is cis gender, so my experience with exercise is essentially one-sided.)

A 'workout' can mean different things to different people. If you choose to spend time moving your body, this can be anything that feels right to you; it could simply be a time to exercise your mind by just sitting and breathing. I feel that we are often led to believe that our workouts must push our limits or suit specific criteria, but we don't have to engage in this biased narrative. In my opinion, it's more about creating the space for you to engage in a liberating, rhythmic activity that frees or builds positive energy and strength, in any way that feels good to you.

I also believe that taking the time to exercise outside is a fantastic way to use working out to connect with the divine! Wiccan foundations lie in nature, but we often forget that we *are* nature! It is within us and everywhere around us – it can be found in a simple house plant, art, the clouds and the sky that surrounds us, whether we live near a forest or in the middle of a city. So even if your hike or workout routine is based in an urban setting, you can still appreciate the clouds, water, birds, squirrels and human nature too! There are also forms of exercise that correlate well with a pagan mindset, such as yoga, Pilates, dance, swimming, hiking and running, as these activities all encourage you to connect with yourself and the world around you. If you already have a favourite sport or exercise that works for you, you could add a magickal emphasis to it to transform the experience.

## PREPARE TO MOVE YOUR BODY

I like to think of the concept of a workout as a personal journey with a start, middle and end. It is almost like casting a circle, performing the spell, and then closing the circle. So, using every little movement to either focus on an intention or move through your journey with spirit is a great way to get through your workout with ease. As with all magick, I encourage you to do whatever works best for you, but here are some ideas for a few different ways that you could prepare for moving your body.

**Hydrate yourself:** make yourself some cleansing water with citrus fruits in it. Lemons, oranges, limes and grapefruit are excellent cleansing fruits with emotional releasing and clearing properties.

**Kit yourself out:** put on some relevant, ritual attire (such as by choosing your gym clothing or putting on some hiking boots); whatever you choose to wear, you're preparing yourself physically for the experience!

**Warm up:** build up your energy by doing some deep breathing exercises.

**Charge yourself up:** if you want a more magickal element to your preparations, you can use some charged moon water to draw a sign onto your stomach or forehead such as this protective earth grounding symbol:

$$\oplus$$

Then sweat it out!

**Get intuitive:** circling back to intuition (as always), use yours to choose what kind of exercise is right for you today. If you have a sport or practice that you specifically enjoy, that's fantastic. But if you're like me and you struggle to stick to one thing (or focus intensely on one type of sport, then give up a week later, when I burn out) try using your intention to choose the activity that you'd like to do, depending on your feelings, requirements and impulses that day. Sometimes, when I lack energy, yoga is perfect. Other days, I feel as though I need fresh air, so I go for a long walk; or if I want to feel resilient, or build energy, I might do strength training. And there are some days that I do nothing at all! It all depends on what you feel is best for you.

## BODY MOVEMENT, ENHANCED BY SPIRITUAL PRACTICE

You can perceive your workout in many different ways. If it involves cardio or breathwork, you could place the intention for your activity to cleanse, dispose of or emotionally release something that you may feel the need to off-load. If you are going for a walk, you might want to set a purpose to connect with nature, to do an active meditation, or to discover something new that day. If you're practising yoga, you could aim for calm or to be more mindful. If your goal is to feel liberation, dance is a beautiful form of self-expression that is wonderful for artistic aims. Swimming is also brilliant for connecting with an intention – repeating a relevant word with each stroke can be incredibly effective.

Setting an intention for your workout will help you to focus and forget about all the other motives associated with exercise. I think it's essential to maintain a magickal state of mind. You can use a journal or Book of Shadows to concentrate on this aspect for each workout session that you do. You can also use exercise to manifest and visualise something into existence. This practice could be placing energy into attracting something, but it can also be to release something. When I was going through EMDR (Eye Movement Desensitization and Reprocessing) therapy, I felt as though I was carrying my realisation of trauma around as a heavy burden, so I started doing light weight lifting. This helped me to feel as if I was charging up with magickal energy, which enabled me to overcome my feelings of fear and lack of control. A sense of accomplishment from a natural, raw form of movement can help you appreciate that healthy change is possible.

# AFTER THE WORKOUT

As I mentioned earlier, the end of a workout is as important as closing the circle within a ritual.

**Note it down:** write about your experience and your evaluations in your journal or Book of Shadows in preparation for your next session. Explain how it made you feel and if there is anything that you'd like to change for the future.

**Close the circle:** think of a word or phrase that you can say either internally or externally once you've finished your magickal movement. A verbal or written affirmation with positive influences is a must-have for me! Writing the words 'I am strong and free' after my workout makes me feel that I have done something worthwhile for myself and my body. Or just one word afterwards such as 'choices' or 'river' can connect you to a calm or uplifting train of thought for the rest of the day.

**Cleanse:** a shower is a perfect way to close a workout. You can visualise yourself washing away everything that you have released or rinsing away anything that you need to. Alternatively, if you want to hold on to a feeling after your physical exercise, visualise the shower charging you with energy!

**Eat:** making yourself a meal or a healthy snack could also be perceived as nourishing or re-fuelling the power that you have burnt.

# REMOVING THE TOXICITY AND NEGATIVE ASSOCIATIONS FROM EXERCISE

Using our bodies in any way that feels good to us should be a celebration of who we are and the amazing potential of physical expression. However, there have been many times that I have primarily associated working out with weight loss, so I've had to refrain from it completely. I have felt that unhealthy motivations to exercise can lead me to a downward spiral of obsessive over-training, calories and obsession with my weight. I don't think exercise needs to be about numbers on the scales, achieving a goal or working towards getting a better booty. Incorporating a spiritual emphasis into my workouts has helped me focus less on the aesthetic results of movement and more on the spiritual, mental and physical health benefits.

I am also aware that many people might not feel comfortable participating in a particular sport or going to the gym, or able to do so. It is essential that when you work out, you feel that you are in a safe place or setting. If you don't have a positive experience somewhere, don't keep returning to this space and hoping that it will work out differently. Finding a situation where you feel protected and free to exercise is more important than pushing yourself to physical goals. Doing what you can once a week, because you love it, is just as good for you and more sustainable than working out every day, robotically, regardless of what the media or society tells you. Your living, breathing body is a beautiful celebration that should be a personal exploration of pleasure. If it's anything different from that or doesn't feel good, it's okay to stop, change, find something new, or do whatever you think is suitable for yourself. If there is no joy or joy to come, there is no point. You must exist for you and you only.

# 8.

# Rest

Sleep and rest are magickal processes. We all need time to wind down and let our intuition guide us to work through the emotions that we store within us throughout the day. Sleep helps our bodies to heal, and our minds to feel relaxed and well. Since I started to prioritise sleep, I have noticed that I always feel at my brightest in the morning and my mind feels clear and positive. This realisation led me to think about how I could introduce periods of rest and repair into my days through meditation, divination and exercise, all of which I have found to be practical go-to tools.

Recently, I read an old journal entry of mine from a difficult time, in which I mentioned that I felt pressure in every area in my life. I felt that stress spread into my work, spirituality and creativity. I even felt pressure to rest and take more time for myself, as well as to spend my downtime reading or completing tasks like cleaning out my cupboards or exercising! I filled my life with a permanent striving to be better or live up to the unrealistic expectations that I felt surrounded me. During my time of awakening, I took a break from work and rediscovered the benefits of rest with meditation, mindful movement and just giving myself space to think. Gradually, conscious relaxation became a crucial part of my life and it enabled me to function in a healthy, calm way. Without any debate, rest is essential for maintaining wellbeing and as a fundamental element of our Wiccan practices.

When you begin your Wicca or witchcraft journey, you may often get caught up in trying to be the most productive Wiccan in order to prove your status in the community, avoid mistakes and educate yourself in the craft. I experienced this on a heightened level, due to the pressure of having an audience on YouTube. This anxiety is becoming increasingly common as we all have access to multiple platforms on which we can share any aspects of our lives. Personally, I wanted to know and experience everything about Wicca and witchcraft in order to help others with their journeys. I now feel that this approach can do more damage than good.

By all means, read, write and educate yourself – but take your time. There really is no rush and a slow, unhurried approach is far more enjoyable. Sharing your journey can be magickal, but to avoid pressure early on in your experiences, only share with people close to you or with Wiccan individuals who you trust and feel safe communicating with. Always remember that mistakes are not a failure; they're simply an opportunity for growth.

Practising Wicca includes spending time connecting to the earth and allowing our minds to heal; without rest, we will become spiritually burnt out. So I would encourage you to free yourself from the perception that your spiritual journey is your identity, forget about labelling yourself a Wiccan, and focus on incorporating practices that will generally improve your life, based on Wiccan beliefs. For example, if you feel your food needs some extra magick, incorporate Wicca into your cooking; if you need better sleep, use spiritual practices such as dream divination to help with that. Maybe if you think that exploring the outside world can help you with what's going on inside, read up on green witchery. We are in this faith to give and receive; the practice of Wicca shouldn't feel like a difficult mountain to climb, or as if you have something to prove. Make the time to rest and really connect with nature.

# SLEEP IS MAGICK

I cannot stress enough that sleep is one of the most essential elements of a healthy mind and is also a fantastic physical, emotional and spiritual healer. The way that our bodies recharge naturally in an unconscious state helps us connect to our subconscious, work through emotions and enter other realms beyond our perception.

Our dreams are truly magickal creations of the human mind and can help us connect to our spirits. I mentioned briefly in the last chapter how, a few years ago, I took part in EMDR (Eye Movement Desensitization and Reprocessing), which helped me deal with some trauma that I had struggled to remember and understand. Throughout this process, which lasted around three to four months, I had the craziest dreams. Every night was like entering a new story, and I felt as immersed in the dream as I am in my daily life. It was an overwhelming but utterly life-changing experience.

In addition to this, it got me thinking about the effects that dreaming can have on our minds and our bodies, as we can process our emotions while we are asleep. My belief is, the more sensitive that you are, the more you typically tend to dream. I dream every night and always have, and when I practise meditation and yoga, I have more or fewer dreams, depending on where I am, emotionally. Dreaming can be incredibly beneficial to you and can also signify that you are feeling happier, excited or fulfilled.

I've kept a dream journal on and off throughout my life, and it has been a helpful way of reconnecting to my thoughts, memories and emotions. But after my experience with EMDR, I started to think about what my dreams were telling me and how I could incorporate that into my magick. I also considered how important sleep was to my general wellness and how I could use Wicca to encourage that overall spiritual recharge. Your sleep state and dreaming can also improve your own connection to yourself and your practices. We can study our dreams for signs to work on specific areas of our lives, for shadow work and to analyse our imaginings and in that way to connect with our subconscious.

## WHAT YOUR DREAMS ARE TELLING YOU – DREAM SYMBOLISM

When interpreting your dreams, try at first to use your intuition to understand what they might mean. Often, their origins are so deeply rooted in our subconscious that a common image or theme may express entirely different things to different individuals.

Particular objects, places, or people can symbolise something specific that's occurred in your life previously or that is happening to you currently.

Our minds will often try to control scenarios by allowing us to re-enter them in our sleep, to gain a sense of peace with our emotions. Try looking for and recording symbols and reflect on what they could represent. For example, if you dream of an isolated house, this could point towards loneliness, isolation and fear of abandonment. Close your eyes, focus on the symbol that you have recorded and allow the associations to flow into your mind. Go with your intuition – you know your subconscious better than anyone!

I believe it's best to try to remain open-minded about whatever your interpretations may be, but if your dream's associations remain a mystery to you, there's no harm in researching others' perspectives on their potential meanings. Here follows a list of some common themes that could come up in dreams and my ideas about what you might want to think about when they occur.

## PLACES, PEOPLE, THEMES

If there are recurring people, places, or themes, try to remember what happened during the day before you had the dream. Did something take place that triggered you towards needing to work through an emotion or pattern of thoughts? It could have been something positive or negative; maybe something that stayed with you on some level after the event, or you might not have given it a second thought until now? Is there something that could do with resolving?

## COLOURS

Colours can represent an array of different emotions, and it is usually best to work out intuitively what tone the colour is setting within your dreams. For example, if your dreams are overwhelmingly dark, you might be struggling with deep anxiety, trauma or buried emotions. This tends to be quite an obvious interpretation, so don't overthink or worry if your dreams are always dark, as your brain might need to find a way to work through your feelings. If you dream in bright fuchsias or purples, this could indicate spiritual insight and the absorption of knowledge. Again – use your intuition to think about what different colours might mean to you; this can be personal to each of us.

## CONTROL AND SUBMISSION

If you often have dreams in which you are entirely in control, and you feel power over a scenario, person, or emotion, this usually indicates progression and healing. However, this explanation might not correlate if you are controlling something or someone from negative motives. This kind of dream doesn't imply that you are a bad person, it's simply your shadow-self being exposed, and it might point towards a familiar and challenging feeling such as jealousy, anger and rage. Take some time to reflect and see where this control is directed and what emotions come with the dream.

If you often lack control in your dreams, or feel others take advantage of you or force you into actions that you are uncomfortable with, take a look at your fears in these scenarios and what specifically makes you feel as though you lack control or power. Does this relate to anything in your personal life? Think about what steps you could take to free yourself from this feeling.

## ANIMALS

The association will be determined by your emotions about the particular animal. For example, you could be scared of what the animal represents, ready to embrace it, look after it or you might be intrigued by it. Examine your feelings towards the animal and reflect on how this might apply to a situation or person in your past or present life. How could you interact with the animal to help resolve or move the situation forwards? You might want to research what the animal represents in ancient Celtic lore or symbology.

## WEATHER

Weather in dreams can indicate a heavy amount of built-up positive or negative emotions. Once again, I encourage you to use your perception to decipher these dreams, but here are some weather states and their general meanings:

- *Light rain*: can indicate a lack of control, destruction, loss, release or letting go.
- *Sunshine*: heavy emphasis on the sun in dreams can mark freedom, liberation, happiness and fortune.

- *Snow*: can represent contrasting feelings – from loneliness, isolation and solitude to calm, healing and peace.
- *Heavy rain*: can indicate catastrophe, anxiety, fear, anger, strength and power.

## EMOTIONS AND FEELINGS

Although this may seem to be an obvious indication, it is essential to look at how you feel in your dreams and whether this reflects something happening in your subconscious mind that you may be ignoring or burying.

## DISTORTION OR IRREGULAR PACE

Your dreams might feel distorted, out of place or stagnant. They may be hurried or accelerated; they might involve jumps to different locations or situations; or you may be experiencing something impossible or that makes no sense in your everyday waking life. This type of dreaming could indicate that you are feeling overwhelmed, but also passion and excitement. From my experience, if you have these sorts of dreams, you typically wake up feeling tired, but also possibly with an overall sense of relief. This feeling of comfort may be because your brain has just released a massive rush of emotions and processed them while you were asleep.

PRACTICAL MAGICK TIP – RECURRING DREAMS

If you have a recurring dream, or themes that appear time and time again, you may want to reflect on what the dream represents in relation to when it occurred. Recording your dreams in a journal comes in handy when tracking back your emotions on the day of the recurring dream. Do your feelings around this time connect with the actions in your dream? Did something trigger it?

If keeping a dream journal feels like too much, write a paragraph about your dreams in your regular journal as a part of your daily journaling. It can be all too easy to end up with at least three separate journals – magickal, dream and daily – that become hard to keep up with!

## CREATE A NIGHT-TIME RITUAL

As we've discussed, when we are asleep our minds can work through our emotions independently of our conscious thoughts. So, if you're not up for analysing what is happening in your dreams, you can create a ritual to help encourage a night of better sleep. You can adapt this depending on what you feel you need, but unless you want to use your sleep for a spell that's not related to rest (for example, solving a daytime problem within a dream), the goal should probably be to wind down to allow your mind to work its magick.

I recommend leaving your phone on silent or placing it somewhere where it won't disturb you until the morning. In the past I have had an issue with being over-attached to my phone, and I am in favour of maximising phone-free time, but if you're worried someone might need you, pop it in your bed-side drawer on vibrate, and you should hear it. There are significant benefits from not scrolling social media before you go to sleep or first thing in the morning. You could try this for a week and see whether you notice any differences in your anxiety levels and your quality of sleep. Social media is incredibly addictive – so you might not find it easy – but it's definitely worth persevering with.

# CALMING NIGHT-TIME SPELLS

Here follow some simple spells that you can include in your night-time ritual whenever you feel the need to.

## CALMING MILKY DRINK SPELL

This spell soothes your mind before you sleep, helping you float into the night, and encourages emotional healing.

**Intent:** For emotional release at night-time.

**Perfect time:** Any time before bed!

**You will need:**

a mug of oat milk (*perfect for grounding and calming; alternatively, use almond, soya or cow's milk*)
1 tsp vanilla extract
1 tsp golden syrup, maple syrup, or honey
paper and a pen
a timer (*your phone will do before you put it out of sight for the evening!*)

*Optional extras*:
a kitchen wand, such as a spoon or teaspoon
your favourite mug

✶ In a saucepan, heat a cupful of milk with the vanilla. If you have a magickal spoon that you like to use, stir the milk frequently, stirring in an anticlockwise direction to activate your milk.

✶ Pour it into your favourite mug and stir in the syrup of your choice.

* Write a calming phrase on a piece of paper. I frequently use:

   *Allow this drink to centre me, and bring me back into my body, which is my home.*

* Fold up the paper and place it under your drink for precisely 1 minute, using your timer. The number 1 is great for spells focused on *you*, allowing the emphasis to be solely on you for a short while.

* After the time is up, take a moment to get comfortable and sip with little or no distractions. Allow the drink to send you into a restful state.

## INNER BREATHING CLEANSE

This quick physical practice uses your *prana* (life force) to cleanse your body and lift the heavy energy that you may have been carrying around with you during the day. This energy can come from anywhere, including trauma and depression, but this spell is to help temporarily lift it so that you can sleep. We often forget that our bodies hold this emotional energy. It can be lightened in many ways, including by eating whole foods, drinking water, minimising the intake of alcohol or toxic substances and practising breathing exercises.

**Intent:** To release heavy energy from the body before bedtime during a time of sadness or discomfort.

Time: Before you go to sleep.

* Start by lying down. You can support your head with a pillow if you wish. Feel free to try different positions to see what feels best.

* Now take a deep belly breath, fully engaging your diaphragm and abdominal muscles. Make the inhalation last for at least 4 to 5 seconds (slowly count up to 5). Then release the breath for around 7 seconds. Wait for 2 seconds, then start over again.

* It's normal to feel a little odd during breathwork practices but stop immediately if you feel *at all* faint.

* Do this between 10 to 20 times, depending on how much energy you feel you need to release, and repeat every night if you need to.

* Once you have finished, lay still for 30 seconds and allow your breathing to return to normal.

## WELL-RESTED CANDLE SPELL

This final ritual is a simple spell using candle magick to help you have a peaceful night's sleep. Performing this spell will allow you to let go of any heavy thoughts or feelings that may be preventing you from getting the sound sleep that you need.

**Intent:** To get a healing night's rest.

**Time:** Tuesday evening – good for overcoming obstacles and protection.

**You will need:**

1 blue candle in candleholder
a pen or some paint
a plate
3 lavender sprigs
lavender essential oil

★ Prepare this ritual half an hour before you go to bed to ensure that you have enough time to allow your candle to burn down completely. You will need to be at your bedside table if possible for this spell.

★ Start by writing or painting the word 'rest' onto your candle. Place your candle in its holder, then place this onto the plate.

★ Take the three lavender sprigs and arrange them on the plate around the candle. Follow this by taking a drop or two of lavender oil onto your finger and drawing a ring around the base of the candleholder to create a magickal seal.

★ Sit on the bed, light the candle, close your eyes and visualise yourself floating in a peaceful dream state. When you have that image in your head, open your eyes and say the words:

> With this candle burn
> and the late-night clock doth turn
> I place my head to rest
> make this sleep my best!

★ Slightly tap each lavender sprig into the flame (without setting fire to them!) and then rub each one onto your pillow.

★ Allow the candle to burn out completely, and NEVER leave the candle unattended or lit when you're going to sleep.

★ Have a good night's sleep!

## RESTING REGULARLY IS ESSENTIAL

Allowing ourselves to have quality rest assists every part of our lives. We must challenge hustle culture if we want a healthier, calmer existence. Not only that, resting and down-time are *natural*. In the Wiccan community, it is recognised that our energy may be lower after spell work, and we will need a good night's sleep and a slow day after we perform particularly intense spells.

The festivals of our yearly wheel acknowledge that we need time to rest. We can also see within our weekly patterns that time to relax is required, so why do we often feel the urge to resist this? Believe it or not, you are not put on this earth to toil until the day you die. You can love what you do, and it's fantastic if you want to spend your spare time working, but balance is always needed. If there is no sense of stability and we find ourselves unable to take breaks, this can often be an avoidance tactic to prevent us from caring for ourselves.

Rest also doesn't just mean watching TV or getting a takeaway instead of cooking. It can mean having a spiritual rest, a day filled with books, calming cups of tea and meditation. Rest should be good for your mind and it should feel appropriate for you! It should be a part of every day, and if you struggle to find some time in the morning to allow your mind to be still, find 10 minutes when you can throughout your day. How are we ever going to learn what we need if we don't have time to reflect on what's happening in our lives?

## CREATE A SPIRITUAL RE-CHARGE DAY

If you work full-time or have responsibilities that leave little free-time, creating a spiritual re-charge day can help during those times when you feel overwhelmed and as though you haven't had a second to yourself.

Some essentials I recommend for a spiritual re-charge day include:

**No technology:** to me, this is really important. When we spend so much of our energy caught up in others' lives or in worldwide issues, we forget what's happening in our own lives. It's only a day, and trust me, you'll want to throw your phone into the sea once you spend a few days without it.

**No pressure:** whatever you do, don't think about achieving anything or completing any tasks. Today is about enjoyment or doing activities that are JUST for you. No other agenda is required.

**A loose plan:** make a plan for what you'd like to take part in during your re-charge day. To some, this may defeat the point, but for me it's an absolute must. Some days, I've planned to wind down and chill out, but I've ended up playing video games, sitting on my phone and feeling emotionally wound-up. I want to encourage you to think about what helps you relax, even though the idea of it might feel like a burden just before doing it. For me, yoga is an absolute *must*; it is my little indulgence. I feel the same about a proper bath, with candles and a cup of tea.

**Solitude:** ideally, it is best to spend a large portion of this day alone, without your partner or family members, if you can. I know this may be difficult, but it's essential just for today to ensure that you don't occupy your spare time primarily caring for everyone else's needs.

**Preparation:** I also try to prepare the night before; I leave out some comfy clothes, my writing, sketching and journaling materials and any books that I fancy reading. I also prepare some easy, healthy meals ahead of the day. This preparation ensures that I don't spend half of my time searching for the things that will help me to relax. The idea is to just *be*, and play a little and rest – with a clear, peaceful mind.

If you take the opportunity to relax and unwind just for a day, you will be a happier, calmer person, which will benefit yourself and everybody around you and help your close relationships flourish.

# 9.

# Intimacy in Wicca

One of the things that initially drew me to Wicca was the open conversation it allows around sex, reproduction and love. I grew up feeling a lot of shame and confusion associated with sex, what it meant to people and why it seemed to mean so much. I never understood why people were called offensive names and were damned for having certain feelings.

So, when I started to learn about Wicca, I felt an immediate sense of peace of mind. Knowing there was an entire holiday dedicated to sexual expression and fertility (Beltane or May Day) made complete sense to me. I loved the idea that sex was natural; after my exposure to the way it is regularly portrayed in the media, it had seemed anything but natural. I loved pleasure; self-pleasure, and with others. I also loved kissing, cuddling and physical touch that wasn't sexual, so finding out that a religion I already felt connected to was sex-positive drew me closer to the practice.

Many of us who, like myself, grew up in the UK don't like to think of ourselves as anything but progressive. Still, from my experience, I feel we are a relatively sexually repressed nation. In education, we don't often explore sex and intimacy ideas outside the typical 'safe sex' talk. Nor do I feel we are as progressive with sexuality and gender identity ideas as we think we are. Unfortunately, because of this, we can often misuse sex and intimacy. Many of us (including myself) have experienced a lot of unhealthy issues and situations. Unfortunately, in the past, this also led me to fear those who are openly sexually liberated. It used to make me angry to consider those who enjoyed sex without shame.

All Wicca teaches about sex is that it's natural because you are a part of nature, whatever you feel about the subject. Sexual expression shouldn't have a hold on us, it should free us, whether we choose to take part in it or not. Within Wicca, the main message is that life is precious and to be enjoyed. Therefore, if you don't want to engage in sex or an element of it, you shouldn't pressure yourself into doing so. At the same time, if you enjoy sex, you should learn to partake in it healthily and free yourself from any toxicity that you have experienced through it.

Wicca views sex in the way that we perceive all actions in life: if it doesn't hurt anyone, then you have free will. This phrase includes consent, mutual enjoyment and choosing not to have sex or misuse the conversation around sex. Sex is also an intense energy exchange. Therefore, the consideration of who you choose to engage with sexually is something I feel should be considered mindfully. Make sure there is *always* open conversation surrounding sex and what the other partner(s) want. I also want to emphasise that intimacy doesn't always have to be sexual, and you can still use it as an expression of liberation and a magickal interaction. Cuddling, kissing, embracing, holding hands, or meditation can all be used in the same way that sex is for magick, if you wish to.

## SEX MAGICK AND ORGASM MANIFESTATION

Most of my partners have not been pagan or interested in taking part in sex magick, so I don't feel that I have enough personal experience to speak about it in-depth. However, I have learnt that it's a positive exchange between two people, usually as an intention-based practice or exchange of energy. Similarly, I have used self-pleasure and orgasms for magick quite a bit.

Masturbation is something I never felt shame about, which is odd considering my warped views on sex while growing up. Masturbation, for me, was always *my* time. I loved exploring myself, I loved the build-up of energy in the body and the release; all of it was great, and I knew what I liked. But I have also loved forms of intimacy with myself that weren't sexual. I enjoy showering, bathing and getting clean. I love massaging myself and applying oil to my body. I even love stroking my hair and giving myself embracing hugs. I don't know where my healthy view on masturbation came from, but I feel it was because this was just for me, and nobody else had any say about what happened or what I did.

When I was around twenty-one, I started to masturbate with magickal intention. After being in relationships where the sex was great, but not necessarily with the right intentions behind it, I began to realise that I was dissociating during sex. This led me to look into sexual healing. I began using orgasms to manifest as a part of my sexual healing. This practice was one of the healthiest ways to manifest through orgasm since I was so comfortable masturbating.

My orgasm manifestation would typically take place where I had a long period to focus. I would treat the situation in a similar way to how I would like to engage in sex with another person. I would light candles, play some relaxing meditation music and get into some nice underwear or something I was comfortable in. I would have no distractions and focus on masturbation and my performing area. Usually, I used my favourite sex toy, which I had blessed and charged regularly. Then I would set the intention, which I would verbally repeat throughout my masturbation until climax. After I finished, I lay there with myself in utter bliss. And it's a very effective way of manifesting, let me tell you!

## CELIBACY

I have also had recent experience of conscious celibacy within a relationship. This was shortly after coming to terms with the fact I had not experienced sex in the healthiest way during my teens. In common with many people, I carried a lot of internalised misogyny, which weighed me down spiritually and emotionally. Without realising it, I often treated my body as a sexual object as I was so used to feeling my main life goal was to impress men. So, my partner and I took a year off from sexual exploration; instead, we focused on spiritual intimacy, and I came to see the value in celibacy for short and longer periods.

My year of abstaining changed my perspectives and how I wanted to engage in sex. First, I have promised myself that I will never participate in sexual activity with anyone that doesn't value me as a person or who treats me like a sexual object. Second, I need to be more assertive when it comes to my boundaries regarding sex and intimacy. Third, when I stopped perceiving myself as a sexual being for a while, I stopped caring so much about what people thought of me and more about how I thought of myself. Lastly, sex just isn't everything. It can be beautiful, and if you are interested in it, then yes, have sex and make it excellent for you. But I also discovered that intimacy is far more important to me, and sex is just a cherry on the top of life, not the main event. We are all sacred, and our bodies are for us to use as we wish. As long as it brings us joy that can last and doesn't damage us in any way, we should be fine.

# Part 3
# Magick for the Soul

# 10.

# Celebrations for the Soul

The Sabbats, or Wiccan holidays, are an excellent time to celebrate the natural world and what each seasonal phase gifts
us. In short, they are a set of eight holidays celebrating the
earth's cycles, as described briefly in Chapter 2. Many of the
Christian holidays that we observe in the UK are based on
pagan holidays (for example, Christmas is based on Yule and
Easter is based on Ostara), but a significant aspect of pagan
holidays is that they focus on nature instead of modern adap-
tions of what it means to celebrate. During each of these
holidays, we partake in activities that are relevant to what is
happening on the earth at that time; we eat seasonal foods,
honour the world and thank our deities. These are the perfect
times to cast more powerful or in-depth spells and to plan for
the season ahead, while also having fun.

However, despite being an expression of joy, occasionally a
holiday can be overwhelming and create feelings of stress or
pressure. While the Sabbats can be a perfect opportunity to
celebrate the earth and those around us within the Wiccan
faith, sometimes we may find ourselves unable to be with
those who love us, maybe surrounded by people who don't
support our beliefs. It is also easy to forget that there are people within our community who suffer from mental health
issues, or busy Wiccans who are parents or carers, or who for

many other reasons might not have the opportunity to set up a ritual, spell, meal, or take part in every Sabbat. In the past, we might not have had positive experiences of these holidays and even have come to dread what they symbolise for us.

I used to feel pressure to enjoy the Sabbats by following all of the Wiccan customs. This isn't a bad thing, as the traditions in the faith are based on nature, which is our biggest healer. But now I've begun to reframe how I spend these holidays. Over the last few years of healing, I have learnt more about the Sabbats than I ever did within my early years as a practitioner. Wicca allows you to create your own traditions and base them on the earth's spectacular cycle, which we can see, feel and truly appreciate. I have found that placing my own personal traditions for each holiday before what I felt was expected of me as a Wiccan has allowed me to celebrate them more intuitively and magickally.

This is one of the reasons that I feel that Wicca fits into my life more authentically than when I tried to keep to a rigorous routine. Of course, I still cast spells, decorate my altar and celebrate traditions that I have loved for many years, but following a more healing route felt vital in my journey. So, as you will see, I will be suggesting that you spend the holidays with a perspective of self-care, while also honouring the established Wiccan customs and practices. If the concept of the Sabbats is new to you, I suggest researching them in-depth before reading this chapter, as we will be focusing solely on an alternative way of celebrating them, with wellness in mind.

## A HEALING GUIDE TO THE WHEEL OF THE YEAR

Before you read this guide, I would like to clarify that this is just my take on this subject. As mentioned, I do not always feel that I have the time or energy to immerse myself in the

Sabbats in a traditional way – and I think that giving yourself the gift of time and kindness is a celebration in itself. It can be interesting to come at this from a different perspective (and I have not often seen this discussed), but I believe we can respect Wiccan customs while also celebrating the Sabbats in ways that work for us. So I would encourage you to have fun with my ideas and create your own magick for each Sabbat.

## SAMHAIN

*'The Sun God is now making his trip to the underworld, where the Triple Goddess swallows him whole and spreads darkness throughout the land. The Triple Goddess now arrives in her Crone phase.'*

Samhain is one of my favourite holidays alongside May Day or Beltane. The amount of power and energy that surrounds the earth on this day is remarkable. Today, the veil has lifted between us and the spirit realm. We celebrate the final turn of the wheel before the cycle starts anew. We celebrate life and death, the circle of life, and honour the dead and our loved ones who have passed on. It's important to remember all of the witches and those people who have been mistaken for witches, whose lives have been lost. We celebrate for them and any other souls that have passed. The darker days have taken over now, and autumn is at its peak.

**Date of holiday:**

*Northern hemisphere:* 31 October to 1 November
*Southern hemisphere:* 30 April to 1 May

**This holiday's main themes:**

- Endings
- The final – and first – turn of the Wheel of the Year
- Death
- The circle of life
- Celebration of darkness
- Celebration of life and death
- Forgiveness
- Acceptance
- Wisdom

**Healing ideas for Samhain:**

**Reflect and mourn:** The summer is primarily a time for action, and the winter is for reflection. The warm weather has passed, and we are left to think and consider our lives and what surrounds us – picking up anything from therapy, meditation, lightwork or other practices that calm us. If we feel we have drifted away from considered goals, or from our truth, now is the time to record this and contemplate.

We can also take this time to mourn. Unfortunately, life can be nonstop and we don't often allow ourselves space to grieve. In contrast, this holiday encourages you to stop and take the proper time to feel your emotions, and whether you are suffering from loss, betrayal, or trauma that might stem from long ago that you may not have been able to process.

**Work with your inner child:** On this day, we celebrate death and life, so what better time to look at the patterns that have been running through our lives since childhood. Samhain is the ideal occasion to connect with your inner child. Do some inner child meditation, journal prompts and divination to help you connect to your intuition (see Chapter 4). This can uncover anything that your inner child might need around Samhain, and try to remember whatever you learn about yourself in the process! This holiday holds an immense amount of high energy, so take your findings seriously and work through them methodically.

**Tap into your intuition:** At Samhain, the Goddess has become older and wiser. We must celebrate this same intuition and wisdom that passes through us all. We each have two sides. One side tends to lead us astray, reacts with fear and confusion and lives in the upper half of our bodies, while the second side lives closer to our root chakra and keeps us grounded, focused and whole. Now is the time to tap into that intuitive, wise, second side by dropping into our thoughts and feelings and bringing that mindset and any hidden boundaries up into our realities for consideration.

## TAROT SPREAD TO ENHANCE YOUR INTUITION

This tarot spread is perfect for honouring the wise Crone aspect of the Goddess that appears during Samhain. It helps you to dig deep into your intuition and strengthen that connection. All five cards should be picked intuitively, based on your energy being drawn towards specific cards. Don't doubt yourself or re-choose.

★ Take five cards. Lay the first two cards next to each other side by side. Then lay the last three cards in a row beneath them.

**Card 1:** What is currently blocking my intuition?

**Card 2:** How can I use my intuition to express myself creatively?

**Card 3:** How can my intuition help me progress my goals?

**Card 4:** How can listening to my intuition help me flourish?

**Card 5:** How can I strengthen my intuition with action?

⋆ Follow this by documenting your results to refer back to when needed.

## A SAMHAIN SELF-FORGIVENESS RITUAL

A lesser-known theme of Samhain is forgiveness, acceptance and letting go. Much like the Death tarot card, we can mourn the loss that comes with endings and celebrate their release and possibilities. Today is the day when we can work with our inner child and shadow self, helping them move forward and forgive ourselves for anything that we struggle to release.

Grief is essential for moving past the feeling of blaming ourselves, which ties in perfectly with this holiday. I developed this simple ritual early on in my healing journey, when I was struggling to forgive my past self. When you're healing, you may go through periods of regret and reflection around your past actions, but guilt is good. It can be used to make sure that you no longer repeat past patterns. However, if you find yourself wallowing in self-regret, this helps no one, nor does it help you move forward and it could be keeping you stuck in your past emotions and thoughts.

This ritual is designed to help you move forward and heal through sigil work. Throughout my Reiki training, I learnt that our stomachs are where we hold the majority of our nervous and guilty energy; hence the gut being the centre of this spell. All of the herbs and colours are tied in with the theme of Samhain to make sure that it sets the correct tone.

Ensure that you won't be disturbed by anyone during this ritual, and enjoy!

**Purpose:** To forgive yourself for past events or forgive past versions of yourself.

**Perfect time:** Best at Samhain!

**You will need:**

rosemary water or water in which rosemary has been soaked for a few days
flowers of your choice
a few fresh or dried bay leaves
1 black candle (*for endings, healing and renewal*)
a forgiveness sigil (*mine is shown below and roughly translates as 'I forgive myself and wish to move on'.*)

✴ Start by preparing a space to lie in. A bed is the most obvious choice. Clean and cleanse the area if you wish; it adds to the self-care element of this spell.

✴ Lay some bay leaves and the flowers out on your bed. Then light the black candle, putting it somewhere safe for the spell's duration.

✴ Lie down in the centre of the flowers and herbs and relax. When you are ready, expose your stomach and take the rosemary water that you have prepared. Dip your fingers in the water and draw the sigil out on your belly three times:

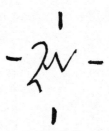

* After each time say the words:

 *I thank the power of Samhain's energy to make a shift within my soul.*
 *I allow myself to move on, forgive my past self and free my present self.*

* Once you have finished this, lie there comfortably and allow the water to dry. Let the candle burn out naturally, and go and make yourself a cup of tea.

## YULE

*'The Sun King returns to warm up the cold earth.'*

Yule is the festival that represents letting go of the old and welcoming the new. This Sabbat is focused on endings, new beginnings and is a great time to rest, recover and look forward to the following year. Now is the perfect time to meditate, manifest, to give to those around you and to make some space with time away from technology. Yule occurs when others might celebrate Christmas. It can be a challenging time for those without a family or support around them, so take care of yourself at Yule, keep warm and create some traditions that bring you genuine fulfilment.

**Date of holiday:**

*Northern hemisphere*: 20 to 24 December
*Southern hemisphere*: 20 to 23 June

**This holiday's main themes:**

- Light returning to the earth
- Celebrating the fertile darkness
- New beginnings
- Reflection
- Giving back to the earth
- Preparation for the new year to come

**Healing ideas for Yule:**

**Giving to or volunteering at a charity**: even though this might not initially seem like the ideal way to spend your holiday; it's a perfect way to end the year with gratitude and a positive exchange of energy. Helping others can be healing for the soul and can give you a healthy and fresh perspective on the earth and how others exist on our amazing planet.

**Take a bath:** this is not a scrolling-through-your-phone bath – leave your phone in another room. Grab some seasonal bubble bath with notes of warming spices to honour the cold that is with us and the warmer days that are to come. Then hop in your bath with your journal, write yourself some journal prompts for the year, and truly unwind and relax. After your bath, give yourself some care with a healing self-massage, thus finishing the evening with some indulgent perfection!

**Bake and create food (with love!):** there are plenty of Yule-related cooking rituals, so why not cook yourself a meal or bake a cake and share it with others – or enjoy it yourself! Either way, fill it with love and use it to honour and nourish your body. Guilt surrounding food can escalate at this time, so remember to stay away from that mentality and allow the earth to provide for your body.

**Create or bake gifts for your family and friends:** there is also immense pressure to spend money during Yule. We can easily be sucked into consumerism, leaving us feeling drained. You could try creating, cooking and baking gifts for your loved ones. Art is therapeutic at any time of year, but even more so as a bit of a rebellion against the consumerism that has taken over celebrations at Yule.

**Make a vision board:** instead of writing goals for your next year, create a vision board of images based on love for yourself, how you would like to feel and new elements that you would like to welcome into your life. I no longer write goals for myself because I don't want to live my life always looking for the next aim or achievement. I now manifest using a vision board based on affirmations and how I'd like to feel. I often write down what I would like to encourage in my life such as moving my body more or welcoming more cruelty-free products into my beauty routine. Instead of manifesting a job that you feel you need to do, re-evaluate and aim for a job that will make you happy! Create a board with pictures of yourself or things that you love and fill it with quotes and affirmations. At the top of your board, create a self-loving mantra for the year, such as 'I will show up as my authentic self in 202X.' Of course, goals are great if you feel they motivate you! Just keep it positive and self-affirming.

## A MINI YULE ALTAR FOR A YEAR OF GROWTH

I created this spell when I fancied doing some manifestation before the New Year started, but I wanted to be creative and make sure my intentions were strong, and that the universe knew that. I recommend relating everything you put into your Mini Yule Altar to what you would like to manifest or relate this to the coming year's goal or mantra. For example, you might put coins in the nest if you'd like to attract financial benefits or a talisman pertaining to spiritual growth if that's your intention for the year. This year, mine included symbols and trinkets for peace and inner calm! You can also choose colours and herbs and their magickal properties to set the tone.

**Intent:** To set a personal intention or manifestation for the year.

**Perfect time:** Either at Yule or the start of a new year.

**You will need:**

air-drying clay in any colour you like
pen and paper
a bowl or plate for the base (*half a coconut shell would be fun!*)
feathers in any colours (*see Chapter 19, pages 216–20 for more on feathers and their meanings*)
dried flowers and herbs of your choice
any trinkets that relate to your intention or goals
	for the year, for example: crystals, talismans
	or coins.

2 spell candles (*choose their colours according to the nature of your intention, or use white, red or green for the winter solstice*)

✶ Start by taking your clay and making a little talisman that resembles you or your soul. For example, I created a womanly shape to capture my essence. It doesn't have to be a realistic likeness; it just needs to feel as though the talisman captures a representation of you.

✶ Place it to the side and allow the clay to dry. Take your piece of paper and write down either your personal goals or your general intention for the year. It can be as simple as writing 'presence' or 'joy' if you don't have specific goals.

✶ Fold up the paper and place it to the side. It's a good idea to make a copy of your goals or intention first, though, so that you have a reminder.

✶ Now is the time to start building the nest in which to lay your figure. Begin by using a plate or a bowl to create a base, then place your paper with your goals or intention at the bottom of the nest.

✶ Put some feathers in there, followed by any dried flowers, dried herbs and then trinkets that you would like to include, slowly building up a little nest until you are happy with it. Take your time and make sure that it feels right to you, as this altar will be with you for a year. It's best not to place anything fresh on the nest that could perish, but you can leave offerings around it throughout the year or on the Sabbats.

✶ After doing this, place your clay figure on the nest, representing you lying within your manifestations for the year.

✶ Position your candles on either side of the altar and light them.

✶ Place your hands on your heart and say the words:

*In this altar, my hopes are planted,*
*within this year*
*my manifestations will be granted.*

✶ Feel these words with all of your soul. Allow your spell candles to burn down completely and keep your mini altar safe for the year; keep it intact but you can move it around, and watch the universe manifest whatever you need!

## IMBOLC

*'The Sun King now comes into his power. The Triple Goddess welcomes us with her Maiden form as she warms up the earth.'*

Traditionally, Imbolc marks the start of the lambing season, when new life and growth begins again. If you live in the UK, the first signs of green life appear around you; the warmth will be here soon. Now is the time to start preparing for the spring. This holiday is also known as Bridgid's Day, as its original purpose was to celebrate the goddess Bridgid! She is the goddess of warmth, fire, the sun, fertility and the hearth, which is very relevant to where we are in relation to the Wheel of the Year. This Sabbat is a beautiful, healing holiday because it is about nurturing yourself, new hope and watching the world come alive after its long sleep. This is the perfect time to make personal plans and to formulate projects, or changes that need to happen this year.

**Date of holiday:**

*Northern hemisphere:* 1 to 2 February
*Southern hemisphere:* 1 to 2 August

**This holiday's main themes:**

- New growth
- The cold earth warming up
- The return of life
- Rebirth and reinvention
- Letting go of the winter months

**Healing ideas for Imbolc:**

**Clear out your home and reorganise:** Imbolc is the perfect time to clean your house of any old energy that may be weighing you down. So much of nature still lies dormant, so you have some time to recollect and then move ahead. First, I would recommend cleaning out any items with negative associations that you may have around, such as pictures, clothing and anything that no longer serves you. Then, follow this clear-out by re-shuffling the energy in your house (see page 180 for cleaning and clearing tips). Doing this at Imbolc is exceptionally uplifting. I've made it a yearly tradition!

**Have an emotional clear-out:** Imbolc is also the perfect time to get the ball rolling with anything spiritual or emotional that you would like to approach. You could start meditating, journaling, planning a new spell, getting your creativity flowing, or even book your first therapy session. So, whatever you've been putting off doing, start now! You will thank yourself later this year.

**Create a simple Self-dedication Candle Magick Spell:** As well as being known as Bridgid's Day, Imbolc is also known as Candlemas. It is a pagan tradition to light candles on this day as a symbol of the flame of Bridgid. This simple ceremony will help bring luck and light to yourself and those around you for the warmer days ahead; candle magick has many purposes! Something I love doing is lighting a pink spell candle, writing myself a self-dedication note, placing it under the candleholder, and burning the candle. Doing this ceremony is a way of dedicating yourself to *yourself* for the year. I typically write some new boundaries that I would like to set or a small phrase such as, 'This year I will make genuine connections.' After the candle has burnt out, keep the note on your mirror as a reminder for the rest of year.

**Go for a walk and take some time to reflect:** Leave your phone at home and take yourself out for a walk. Have a look for the first signs of spring, notice life emerging, bulbs poking through the soil, early honeybees around crocuses and ladybirds on a sunny day. Use this to inspire thinking about how your life could create new growth this year.

**Journal:** Create and complete some journal prompts around the idea of what you would like to release yourself from this year and of what you would like to invite into your life. If not, feel free to use mine (see below)!

---

PRACTICAL MAGICK TIP – IMBOLC JOURNAL PROMPTS

Here are five short journal prompts that tie into the themes of Imbolc. As someone who journals daily, I like to incorporate these into my mornings at this time of year.

- How can I encourage inner growth this year?
- What did I learn this winter that could help me in the coming year?

---

- What makes me feel alive right now? How could I incorporate that feeling into my daily life?
- Picture Bridgid in your mind; what does this image represent for you and what is it trying to tell you at this current moment?
- Write a short love letter to the universe, describing where you'd like to be this summer and what you'd like to be doing.

## AN IMBOLC JAR SPELL TO RELEASE THE WINTER BLUES

For this spell, we are bringing everything that we can to enable us to let go of those elements of our lives that are holding us back. These are not just factors that are relevant to the winter. You have to truly welcome letting go and acceptance into your being for this spell. Release anything that's happened (or capture that energy) and be ready for new beginnings and change. The universe knows if you're not using self-dedication to make this work! So, save an entire evening for this spell and bring out all the intention and energy that you can! It perfectly symbolises letting go of the cold and welcoming in the warmth.

**Intent:** To let go of the past and move forward with good energy.

**Perfect time:** Imbolc evening.

**You will need:**

1 yellow candle
a stone

small amount of yellow paint and a paintbrush
pen and two small pieces of paper
1 medium-sized jar with lid (plastic if you don't want to freeze
    a glass jar)
table salt (*you are going to need a lot!*)
handful of dried thyme
handful of dried rosemary
handful of dried lemon balm, or fresh or dried lemon pieces
    (*any of these will work!*)
yellow ribbon
1 lepidolite crystal or a crystal that you have chosen
    intuitively

✴ Start by cleansing the area that you will be working in by clearing and cleaning space at a desk or altar, and gathering the items listed above. Cast a circle if you feel that you need to, by calling in deities associated with the cardinal points of the compass or the elements of Earth, Air, Fire and Water (see page 39, where I describe casting a circle to consecrate creative tools).

✴ When you are ready to begin, light the yellow candle.

✴ Prepare your sigil stone by cleaning and drying it. Paint this sigil onto it with the yellow paint:

The sigil translates as: 'I let go of the cold I carry. I release it and welcome warmth into every bone of my body.'

✴ While the paint is drying, take one small piece of paper and write down whatever you're carrying with you that you'd like to release. Fold this paper up as small as you can, and then drip some wax on it to seal the paper; no worries if it doesn't seal properly or if it comes open. Your intention is all that matters!

* Place your piece of folded paper at the bottom of the jar. Take your salt and fill the jar to about halfway.

* Place some lemon balm or dried lemon slices around the inside of your jar, leaving the centre of the salt exposed. If you're using fresh lemon, squeeze some juice into the jar.

* Take your rosemary and thyme and do the same thing, creating a nest inside the jar, leaving some space in the top for your sigil stone.

* Then, on your second piece of paper, write why you want to complete this release and how it will help you to move on. The note doesn't have to be long – just a sentence will do the trick! Fold up this piece of paper and seal it again with the candle wax.

* Place the second piece of paper into the jar and place the sigil stone on top of it.

* Screw on the lid and then tie some yellow ribbon around it with the bow at the top of the jar.

* For the night of Imbolc, place your jar, with your crystal on top of it to charge it, either on a windowsill facing the moon or outdoors where it won't be disturbed.

* In the morning, take your jar, place it at the back of your freezer, and leave it there until next Imbolc, when you can either throw it away or revisit what you needed to release a year ago.

* If anything happens to your jar; no worries! Your intention is out there, and the universe has dealt with it. But if you do

remove the jar yourself, empty the contents somewhere safe and burn the two pieces of paper or throw them away, it doesn't matter which! You can cleanse and reuse the jar and keep the sigil stone to remember that you are healing.

# OSTARA

*'The Sun God and the Maiden are now married and will soon become pregnant with the seeds of the earth.'*

Ostara is the celebration of the start of spring, the nights and days are perfectly aligned, and light will take over from now on until autumn. So it's a perfect moment to raise vitality a little bit and focus on moving forward. The winter has officially finished, so you can go full steam ahead into the year. It is great to start spending time outside in the mornings and organising yourself to ensure that you have enough energy and are able to focus on doing the things that you really would like to do this year. Traditionally, Ostara is associated with fertility; plants are in bud everywhere, animals are producing their offspring and eggs symbolise this holiday.

**Date of holiday:**

*Northern hemisphere:* 19 to 22 March
*Southern hemisphere:* 19 to 22 September

**This holiday's main themes:**

- Balance (the earth is in perfect harmony)
- Light is taking over darker days from now on.
- Beginnings
- Plans can begin to come to fruition
- Start of the fertility season
- Life begins in the natural world

**Healing ideas for Ostara:**

**Gardening:** Why not create a magickal herb garden, or an indoor garden? Nature is the most healing presence that we can experience as humans. Its gifts are a right that we should all have access to. Spending your spare time taking care of the natural world is a meditative practice in the rawest form. Not only will this activity connect you to the plants that you are growing, and possibly consuming, and the earth, but it will help you to remain balanced and to feel grounded at this time, fitting the theme quite nicely! You could plant some seasonal herbs outside or grow a few plants inside and they can be there for you to nurture during the year to come. Alternatively, pop to the shops and grab yourself some seasonal flowers to treasure!

**Craft:** Creativity is also amazingly healing, and during this time, there are plenty of crafts associated with Ostara that you can take part in. For example, you could create candles in the shape of eggs or make papier mâché flowers of different sizes and decorate them. You could paint a picture that represents the earth now and symbolises welcoming light to the world, or an image of the new growth that's happening around us. There are many fantastic options if you're looking for a healthy distraction to help you enjoy this holiday.

**Have a 'warmth welcoming' bath:** Grab some fresh, skin-friendly flowers such as roses, daisies, lavender or chamomile, some citrus essential oils, along with some pastel-coloured candles, and run a blissful, warm bath. This is a perfect way to honour yourself and the warmth returning. Place the petals of the flowers in the tub, along with a few drops (only a few) of essential oil, and light the candles. Take this time to relax and re-balance your mind.

**Spring clean!** I mentioned earlier that Imbolc is the perfect time to clean out the old, but this is really relevant to Ostara too! It's not too late to deep clean the house or have a clear-out if this felt too overwhelming at Imbolc. Feel free to open the windows and allow the old energy to leave your home as the weather warms up!

**Perform a self-alignment ceremony:** Balance is a central theme of this holiday, so now is a good time to participate in balancing activities, such as meditation, yoga and any craftwork that helps you feel grounded. This ritual is fantastic if you are struggling to find stability and equilibrium at this time.

PRACTICAL MAGICK TIP – A SELF-ALIGNING CEREMONY

For this small ceremony all you need is a pendulum. Start by standing straight against a wall where you won't be disturbed, holding your pendulum in your left hand until needed.

Close your eyes and picture a seed growing from the top of your head, with the roots extending down into your neck, shoulders, arms, etc. Once the roots reach your feet, picture them growing into the ground and hold that energy there for a few minutes.

Open your eyes and hold your pendulum directly in front of you. If the pendulum swings from side to side, you're out of alignment and change needs to be made. If the pendulum is still, you're good to go.

If relevant, I recommend documenting why you may

feel out of alignment and anything that is happening emotionally for you or around you that might be making you feel that way. Repeat this practice when you feel that you need to.

## AN OSTARA ABUNDANT GROWTH RITUAL

As the warmth returns to the earth with the Ostara sun, it's time to plant our foundations and put everything into moving forwards into the summer months. Set an intention focused around growth or healing and watch it ripen and flourish.

**Intent:** To attract what you need into your life, creating abundance and joy.

**Perfect time:** For best results, perform on Ostara, though any days when the warmth makes an early appearance will work.

**You will need:**

a pot or a patch of garden in which to grow your plant(s)
soil
seeds of your choosing (*be sure to grow something seasonal that you will be able to maintain and take care of for its natural lifespan*)
gardening tools
a label to mark your specific plant with a message (optional)

★ Gather what you need and start by filling your pot with soil. Be sure to research what's best for your plant for the optimum results!

* Before you plant your seeds, hold them in your hands and visualise them growing into magnificent, leafy, healthy plants. Envisage that this represents your growth, too, so send it all the energy, love and luck.

* Place the seeds in the pot, cover them with soil, and say the words:

  *I plant these seeds to attract growth, love, and abundance to my life. So allow me to receive abundance, luck, love and the lessons I need to continue receiving joy in my life.*

* If you wish, you could set a more specific intention by writing it on a label and then pushing this into the soil, and then you can leave it on a windowsill or outside, depending on the plant, and watch it blossom!

* Try to take good care of your plant through its natural lifecycle. However, if for some reason, it doesn't thrive, don't worry! There may be something blocking this growth that you need to re-evaluate. Once you have overcome this, change will be on the way.

## BELTANE

*'The Horned God and the Maiden are now united, bringing new life to the earth.'*

Beltane, or May Day, celebrates the peak of spring. It's a beautiful day to honour sexuality, abundant growth and fertility. Overall, it is a joyous, high-energy Sabbat for many Wiccans. The earth is pregnant with possibilities, both in the physical world and metaphorically. Beltane is my favourite holiday, as I feel my energy is high, and significant transformations take place around this time. However, I can see how this holiday could be challenging for some practitioners. Those with fertility problems, issues associated with the womb, or those who may have lost someone around this time, could find this celebration difficult. As Wiccans, we are taught to honour all of life's gifts and grievances. Still, a part of that celebration is allowing ourselves to feel, whatever those emotions might be.

A few years ago, I decided to make this a time of self-transformation for myself, using the high energy that surrounds us in every living thing. Sex is a beautiful thing, and if you enjoy it, learning to have sex consciously and exploring your sexual self can create healthy boundaries, both within ourselves and with others. But you do not have to be a sexual person to enjoy this holiday! You can embrace the earth's energy at this time and harness your power from that vitality without making it all about sex. Fertility, too, isn't all about sexual practice; it's about possibility and new life. You may want to engage in some healing ceremonies such as crystal healing, sexual healing, safe body exploration, or green/garden magick during this time.

**Date of holiday:**

*Northern hemisphere:* 30 April to 1 May
*Southern hemisphere:* 31 October to 1 November

**This holiday's main themes:**

• Honouring the life around us
• Love
• Sex and passion
• Celebrating our sexuality
• The peak of spring
• Growth
• Abundant fertility, including the pregnant earth

## Healing ideas for Beltane

**Activate your energy:** Activate your life force and enhance your energy through dance, exercise, yoga practice, breathwork, active meditations or Reiki to raise your vibrations with the power of this Sabbat.

**Celebrate your sexuality**: This may seem like a given, but today is the day to celebrate your sexuality. This may not be possible for everyone, but doing something as minor as wearing a badge expressing your pride or journaling positive affirmations are small but excellent ideas. Just to let yourself know it's okay to be you!

**Give yourself a loving massage:** This practice is beautiful for raising energy. Massage is something I feel we should be taught to do from a young age. Touch is such an essential aspect of our being and how we communicate to ourselves and others. If we have experienced negative forms of touch, introducing a self-massage routine into our lives can be immensely healing. The concept of massage has often been misunderstood, possibly coming from the warped view that some people hold surrounding touch and the perception that all intimacy is sexual. Safe touch is overlooked when it comes to healing, and when you allow it to be introduced into your life, this can have an incredibly positive effect on your body and mind. On Beltane, have a lovely bath, dry yourself off, and grab your favourite lotion or cocoa butter and massage your entire body. Slowly explore what you like and what you don't, and allow yourself time to feel refreshed and balanced.

**Work with the shadow self**: Engage with your shadow self during this time. To fully love, cherish and harness our power to work on the things that we want, we must embrace our entire self, including the inner child and the shadow self. First, write some journal prompts (or use mine below) and use these to discover what might be holding you back. In order to let ourselves move beyond the shadow, rather than removing it, we often need to acknowledge it fully instead. Then your shadow self won't control you, but be a fully embraced part of your wonderful being.

---

PRACTICAL MAGICK TIP – BELTANE SHADOW-SELF JOURNAL PROMPTS

Here are some journal prompts that will help you to connect with your shadow self now and throughout the year.

- What is something that others do that you consider to be annoying or frustrating?
- Which actions or traits in others tend to irritate you immediately or become an issue quickly? (Jealousy, competitiveness, attachment, expectations, etc.)
- Do any of these pet peeves reflect something that has happened to you in your life?
- What do these emotions or feelings hold you back from doing?
- What don't you like about yourself and why?
- Now write a paragraph on how you might overcome these things, either with practice or choosing to let something go. Move forward with something you have been putting off because of your insecurities, pent-up emotions or fears.

---

# CRYSTAL HEALING RITUAL FOR IGNITING WOMB ENERGY

This ritual involves lying down between two candles to ignite womb energy.

**Intent:** To heal and ignite womb energy.

**Perfect time:** For best results, perform at Beltane, though other times of the year will work too.

**You will need:**

2 pink candles or tea lights
3 crystals (intuitively chosen)

✴ On the floor, place one pink candle above where your head will be and one below where your feet will be. *Please place the candles safely,* far enough from your head and feet positions so that you won't knock them over while lying down or getting up. Alternatively, you could use tea lights in saucers as these are very stable.

✴ Take the crystals, lie down and place them in an inverse triangular formation where your womb energy flows (below the belly button).

✴ Next, place your hand on your heart and lie there for 10 minutes with your eyes closed. Now visualise a warm healing light traveling from your heart to your womb.

## BELTANE ENERGETIC WOMB RELEASE

This practice is very effective for women or those with a womb who may have health issues or have experienced trauma in this area, including abortion, miscarriage and sexual trauma. Even if you haven't been through one of these experiences, this is an amazingly freeing practice. We are often told not to feel or express anger about things that have happened in our past, even within a spiritual context. To me, this seems counter-intuitive. Spirituality, including within the Wiccan faith, has to include self-acceptance. If anger is there, we can't hide from it or try to suppress it. It needs to be released and maybe even transformed into something that can be beneficial for us. So today, I encourage you not to be quiet or convenient but to honour yourself and your anger with all of your heart. This ties into Beltane, not only in regards to it being a time for sexual healing but also because we are using our life force and uplifting ourselves, transforming that stagnant energy into a blossoming, beautiful power, aligning ourselves with what the earth is doing too. You can perform this powerful practice inside or outside, and feel free to adapt it to whatever feels right for you.

**Intent:** To release heavy energy from your womb.

Perfect time: Beltane or on a Sunday.

✳ Start by finding a place to lie down or to sit upright but with your feet planted on the ground. Place your legs in front of you, a little apart or crossed depending on what feels comfortable. You could even stand up if you wish. Sitting up against a tree is perfect if you're doing this outside!

✳ First, take both your hands and rub them together for a few seconds to generate energy. Then place both of your hands over your lower stomach, supporting and protecting that area of your body.

✱ Take five deep breaths, as deep as you can, in and out. While doing this, focus on breathing into your womb area and root chakra, the energy centre at the base of your spine. Direct the energy and breath there.

✱ Once you have built up the energy, breathe out upon your sixth breath and let out the noise '*haaa*' for as long and as loudly as possible.

✱ In this way, release the heavy energy from your womb space and repeat as many times as you are able. Try to do this louder, more weirdly, and more enthusiastically with every '*haaa*'.

✱ You can repeat this practice whenever you want. I use this if I ever feel triggered or can sense the arrival of trauma, releasing what needs to be removed so I am no longer carrying that pain within.

## LITHA

*'The Triple Goddess and the Horned God are now pregnant, getting ready to bear us gifts in the autumn.'*

Litha is the celebration of the longest day and the shortest night of the year, also known as the summer solstice. It's a beautiful time to celebrate abundance, the sun and the bustling energy that the earth has created. This time can be symbolic for many reasons. It's a wonderful time to focus on growth and love, to use the sun's power to move forward and maybe even for banishing magick and spells.

**Date of holiday:**

*Northern hemisphere:* 20 to 24 June
*Southern hemisphere:* 20 to 24 December

**This holiday's main themes:**

- Growth
- Self-love and love for others
- The sun
- Abundant earth and abundant joy
- The green earth

**Healing ideas for Litha:**

**Take part in sun meditation:** There are a few ways
that you can do this: visualise the sun while
meditating and honour it with your thoughts or
wake up early when the sun is rising and meditate
for around 20 minutes and document anything that
may have come up during the meditation. You can
also do the same in the evening when the sun is
setting. This meditation is a magnificent way to
appreciate the day while also giving yourself some
healthy space.

**Honour your light:** Take some time on this day to write
affirmations for yourself, some personal goals, or
something that you would like to work through. This
Sabbat is the perfect time to let yourself know that
you are lovely. So big yourself up today, dress in
your favourite clothing, wear flowers in your hair,
and embrace your beauty in every way.

**Free up your life:** Use this time to cleanse anything
from your life that needs to be removed. During this
time, the sun is at its peak. You can use its power to

cleanse or metaphorically burn anything out of your life that you don't need anymore. If I'm unsure about what needs to be removed, or if I feel as though the answers to this are hidden from me, I like to use a tarot spread to make sense of my thoughts. Alternatively, you can use a journal or write what needs removing on a piece of paper and burn it (safely). After that, take steps to ensure that the issue won't come back!

**Nourish yourself with seasonal fruits:** Pick locally grown strawberries, raspberries and other seasonal fruits that take your fancy and have a Litha fruit picnic surrounded by nature.

## LITHA TAROT SPREAD

Use your favourite tarot or oracle cards and your intuition for this simple spread and then make a note of the cards' meanings in your magickal journal or Book of Shadows.

**Intent:** To know what needs removing from your life and what needs nurturing.

**Perfect time:** Best at Litha!

For this simple spread, prepare your work area and then pull your cards intuitively from the deck as follows:

**Card 1:** Lay your first card facing you in the centre of your work area. This card poses the question: *What needs changing in your current circumstances?*

**Card 2:** Lay your second card to the left side of the first one, beginning to make a T-shape with your cards. This one answers the question: *Why is this situation/ person/obstacle holding you back?*

**Card 3**: Lay your third card underneath the first card. This card answers the question: *What do you need to nurture?*

**Card 4:** Lay your fourth card on the opposite side to the second card, completing the T-shape. This card answers the question: *Are your next steps moving you forward?*

## LITHA RITUAL TO ATTRACT EXCITEMENT IN THE LAST OF THE SUMMER DAYS

As we welcome the darker days that will now be returning, this is a quick spell to start attracting fun into your life. Of course, only a tiny percentage of how happy we feel depends on what we are doing at that moment. I think that living your life at a fast pace, jumping from one experience to the next, doesn't bring happiness. For me, it is about healing and finding a healthy pace so you can adapt and adjust; it is not about indulgence but considering the bigger picture and dedicating yourself to yourself.

Presence and wholeness are essential, but sometimes it may feel boring to stay grounded all of the time; what you need is balanced and healthy, enjoyable fun! This spell will start to attract whatever fun you have in mind, so make sure that the pleasure that you are seeking is not damaging to your healing. This includes classic number and herbal magick to attract fun for seven weeks after the initial week-long spell.

**Intent:** To attract fun or exciting experiences into your life.

**Perfect time:** Start on Litha day and finish a week later.

You will need:

7 dried hawthorn berries (*or juniper or elderflower berries*)
1 small piece of carnelian (*or other joy-attracting crystals*)
pinch of dried lavender
a small piece of paper with 'I attract fun and exciting
    experiences' written on it
a small pouch or drawstring bag

✴ Place the ingredients including the folded piece of paper
   into your drawstring bag on a Sunday evening and carry it
   around until the following Sunday.

✴ At the end of the week, place all the ingredients, except the
   crystal, into a dish and burn them. Watch exciting experiences attract themselves to you during that week and for
   the next seven weeks to come!

✴ Keep the crystal as a pick-me-up for when you want to
   attract some fun.

## LAMMAS

*'The Sun God is now starting to lose his power, preparing to
sleep for the winter months. So the form of the Triple Goddess has changed again, becoming the Grain Mother,
providing for the earth.'*

Lammas is the Sabbat between the transition of summer
into autumn. The world's growth is slowing down, and this is
the first celebration of the harvest season, followed by
Mabon. We are honouring the harvest with overall themes of
gratitude, abundance, reflection, and the sacrifices we have
made and those that the earth has made for us. The land is
transforming, and so are we. Now is the time to cast spells

associated with protection and change. It is important during this holiday to observe and be thankful for what you have and give back to the earth wherever you can.

**Date of holiday:**

*Northern hemisphere:* 1 August
*Southern hemisphere:* 1 February

**This holiday's main themes:**

- Gratitude
- Abundance
- Giving thanks to the earth
- Change
- Physical, spiritual, and emotional shifts
- Welcoming darkness

**Healing ideas for Lammas**

**Gratitude journaling and living gratefully:** Yes, of course, sometimes finding gratitude can be challenging, and I know I sometimes find it hard to be appreciative for what I have, especially when I am feeling low or depressed. Yet I do think that we all have something to be thankful for, whether it be a lunch that we have eaten, the partner we share our lives with, or the harvest that provides us with food. Lammas shows us gratitude in the purest sense and reminds us to be constantly thankful for what we have and warmed by what the holiday represents. So, I suggest writing down a list of things that you're thankful for today and maybe taking the time to manifest something that you will be grateful for in the future.

As well as expressing gratitude, walk through your daily life with appreciation too. For example, practise mindful eating, take some time to observe the earth before it becomes darker and colder again, and enjoy this day. It is easy to become caught up in your own negativity. Try to take notice of the good that exists beyond yourself every day. Being outside and seeing other people laughing together and appreciating their close connections brings me joy.

**Volunteer or give**: As well as gratitude, we are also celebrating life and death at Lammas. Sacrifice is a challenge that we all face and is a theme of this holiday. Volunteering creates a balance with gratitude and inner hope, so maybe look into giving your time or skills this Lammas or simply choose to give whatever you are able. Bake your friend a cake, help someone out with a task that is easier with another pair of hands or write a few messages to your family, letting them know how much you appreciate them. Acts of service without expectation can be highly beneficial to you and have the extra bonus of giving others a boost, which could be very much needed.

**Finish or release something:** An action that I often see related to this time is 'finish a project'. I completely agree, as this can be satisfying, so if you have anything in your life with loose ends that need tying up, then this is the perfect moment. Alternatively, there might be something that you want to give up, such as a habit that's not working for you, a relationship, negative energy, or even an emotion or feeling. In that case, Lammas is the perfect time. So, take action, cleanse and move forwards!

**Food magick:** Now is the time to transform the earth's generous gifts into tasty food that helps to nourish our bodies. I encourage you to celebrate this holiday without any guilt and shame surrounding your food. Adding magickal intention behind your meals is a beautiful way of giving them meaning and purpose. It can inspire us to try new things, nurture our bodies, and set intentions for the winter months.

## LAMMAS PRAYER

This is a short prayer to sing or speak on Lammas night to honour the Sabbat and bring protection for the winter months.

*I welcome Lammas with all my soul
as the wheel turns again;*

*The fruits of our labour appearing now
from the seeds that we have sown;*

*The Goddess in her bounty is ready to
guide me again;*

*As the days will now grow shorter
from Mabon and through Samhain,*

*Where she will complete her journey
and come to rest at Yule;*

*With the aid of the earth's protection,
let winter be joyous and full.*

## MABON

*'The sun god has taken his rest, along with the goddess. The Green man sacrifices himself to the earth and lays down, ready for his seeds to once again be sown in spring.'*

Mabon is the second Sabbat to celebrate the earth's harvest and we commemorate the days being at perfect balance once again this year. It's time to plan, organise and create stability in our lives; once again, equilibrium is an element of this holiday. Cooking spells are fantastic to do at Mabon, so I've included my favourite Vegan Buttermilk Bread recipe, if you fancy baking something simple but tasty.

**Date of holiday:**

*Northern hemisphere:* 21 to 24 September
*Southern hemisphere:* 21 to 24 March

**This holiday's main themes:**

• The golden harvest
• Grounding
• Stability
• Abundance
• Balance

**Healing ideas for Mabon:**

**Practise breathwork:** Mabon is the time for balancing techniques, so any mindful craft or repetitive exercise will be helpful to prepare for the winter months. Meditation is always beneficial, no matter how you are feeling, and breathwork is another practice that fills us with energy and helps to ground us (see Chapters 3 and 8 for more on these).

**Make a change to your environment or space:** You can make a significant change, such as moving, cleaning and reorganising or cleansing your home, or it could be as simple as just leaving the house for the day. Mabon is about thanking the earth, gaining perspective and grounding yourself, taking yourself outside your comfort zone, and having a day just for you.

**Prepare yourself for the darker days:** Something I never really thought about in my early years as a Wiccan was preparing myself for the more challenging times. I try to live in the moment the majority of the time. Still, I never really realised there was an element of preparation in all of the Sabbats, along with the balance of being present while also looking forward. So now is the time to prepare for the colder days and how you can make things easier for yourself. If you know you struggle with something, particularly during the colder months, reflect and then get organised with any necessary tools to help you through the times ahead. It could be planning a workout routine, buying a SAD lamp, or writing a list of things to turn to when the winter blues get to you. Whatever you choose to do, ensure that it's beneficial and use it as your anchor.

**Get a spiritual haircut or reshuffle your clothing:** This activity may sound completely random, but it is a beautiful time for physical transformations. Even though I always like to encourage the idea that you are great just the way you are (you are a miraculous product of nature!), sometimes it's great to experiment creatively with clothing. It's also a fantastic time for spiritual haircuts, restyling or trims, to shed or sacrifice the old and make room for the new energy during the winter.

**Make a sacrifice:** Mabon is also a wonderful time to give something up in order to make room for the new. For example, you could decide to hold off on consuming materialistic possessions or give up meat and dairy or processed food for some time. This can also cross into the concept of surrendering something that you feel is holding you back, making room for new opportunities.

## MABON VEGAN BUTTERMILK BREAD AND PROTECTION CHARM

This Vegan Buttermilk Bread recipe is a classic charm that I created and uploaded to my YouTube channel in 2018. I wanted to record it in this book as it's a beautiful charm for your peace of mind and will fill your belly with yummy bread. Both healing and tasty! It is also excellent to share with loved ones.

**Perfect time:** Best around 11 a.m. on Mabon.

**You will need:**

700g (25oz) strong white bread flour
500ml (17fl oz) soya milk
2 tbsp lemon juice
1 tsp bicarbonate of soda
a few handfuls of dried fruit (e.g. apricots, raisins and ginger)

*Optional extras:*
green sage
candles and music
Mabon-coloured ribbon or string (brown, red, gold, etc.)

✳ Start by creating a calming environment. Maybe cleanse your kitchen with some protective herbs such as green sage, and create a warming ambiance using candles and music if you wish.

✳ Put your flour, bicarbonate of soda and dried fruit in a bowl and mix it up lightly.

* Then mix your soya milk and your lemon juice in a jug and leave this to sit for five minutes. This process will curdle your milk and replicate 'buttermilk' but it's vegan!

* Once ready, slowly add your buttermilk to the dried ingredients, and mix. You don't have to knead this bread. Just make sure the flour is combined and the mixture isn't too sticky. Feel free to add more flour if it feels too wet.

* Place your dough onto a floured board, press into a spherical shape, and score with a knife into eight cross-sections to represent the year's wheel.

* Line a baking tray with baking parchment and place your bread onto the tray.

* Bake the bread at 180°C (350°F) for 30 to 40 minutes. Keep checking it as you go, and be sure it's cooked in the middle; depending on how good your oven is, it may need longer!

* When you can smell your bread cooking, pop yourself down near the oven and say the words:

    *Mabon have the warmth of this offering –*
    *protection and fullness*
    *from the fields around us.*
    *The winter months through cold and darkness*
    *will be guided through the wheel of the year.*

* Once the bread has baked, leave it to cool. Then take your ribbon and tie it around the bread and into a bow. While you're tying the ribbon, say the words:

    *Grain of bread, protect my space,*
    *my family, my friends, and myself.*
    *Allow the hearth to be full at fall,*

*until light returns at yule*
*So mote it be.*

Voilà!

## CELEBRATE YOURSELF WHENEVER YOU CAN

The Sabbats can be an excellent excuse for self-celebration, but this should be introduced as a part of your daily life, to help improve your overall wellness and your self-esteem. It's lovely when people around you want to honour you, but that might not happen very often. You need to be the source of magick in your own life. Wicca is the perfect excuse to celebrate yourself every day and to take part in the magick that serves you!

I try to celebrate myself for the little things, whether achieving a personal goal or just getting through a difficult day. I honour myself by cooking excellent food just for me, giving myself some personal space to have a nice bath, or watching an indulgent film. On my birthdays I bake myself cakes and take myself shopping.

The way you live your life, talk to yourself and the people and environment that you choose to surround yourself with all have a knock-on effect on your inner voices and how you relate to yourself on a daily basis. This accumulates and makes a huge difference to your emotional wellbeing, so take the little victories and choose to show yourself some love every single day of your life.

# 11.

# Creating a Self-love Altar

A witch's altar is a sacred space that traditionally is used as a safe place to practise magick. It usually occupies a small area, somewhere relatively private, where you won't be disturbed. The conventional perception of an altar might be a table or board set up with magickal items, a pentagram, a divination tool and an object that honours a deity. This setup is all well and good, but where, at this altar, are you honouring yourself?

To some people, this concept may seem daunting, or even disrespectful. When I first had this idea, I thought to myself, 'I am not as great as the earth, nor higher than the power of the universe', and no, I'm not – but I am an equal part of this earth, as are you, too. You deserve to be loved and honoured as much as the next person, tree or season does. A huge part of learning to love yourself and creating wellness in the everyday is realising that you deserve honouring. Trust yourself to know that you have worth and that you deserve a magickal life. It is important to create an altar with all of the traditional elements that it *should* have, such as candles to represent the gods and goddesses, an offering plate, a wand and a bell, but it is also essential to make an altar that *you* want to be at. Without the connection to your sacred space, you might as well use it as a place to store your tools!

When I was struggling with my craft, I could tell that the universe knew that my heart wasn't in it. I lacked so much love for myself, and it was showing within my spellwork. When I started to heal and be kind to myself again, my magick improved profoundly. Creating a self-love altar is a beautiful way to honour yourself, your magick and let the universe know that you're ready for whatever you are asking of it. If you don't, subconsciously, believe that you are worth nurturing, this will weigh heavily within you and show in everything that you do. Of course, creating a self-love altar won't solve that issue, but the transformation is a step towards knowing that you deserve to celebrate and love yourself.

## CREATING YOUR SELF-LOVE ALTAR

When creating your altar, you can still include traditional elements with a little reorganising. Or you can set up a completely different sacred space just for you, somewhere else in your home. I recommend beginning by giving your altar a refresh and making the added self-love elements a permanent addition. I could suggest many beautiful things that you can include, but instead, I believe that putting together your self-love altar should come from your intuition.

### FIRSTLY, THINK ABOUT WHAT REPRESENTS YOU

Which colours do you *truly* love, and which ones are you really drawn to? I added pink wherever it worked for me. Pink represents self-love and is typically a colour that I shy away from because of its overly feminine associations. You could include coloured candles, ribbons, altar cloths, etc., to add a pop of colour. Consider whether there are any trinkets that you would like to incorporate to represent your values. Maybe an animal that you associate with or a yonic painting or sculpture to help heal or honour your yoni? Perhaps a master crystal that you constantly find yourself gravitating towards or something else along these lines?

## WHAT WOULD YOU LIKE TO HONOUR?

Personally, I always struggled to honour and embrace my femininity. In the past, I put men and the masculine upon a pedestal, so I wanted to place the feminine divine up there instead on my altar. So I added some postcards of Botticelli pictures that represent female liberation and empowerment to me, along with ornaments and a candle shaped like a female body that I could relate to. It felt so beautiful to celebrate myself in this subtle way. So ask yourself, what would you like to honour? Feminine, masculine, NB, or other energies? Maybe a deity that symbolises self-love, or something that represents elements that you might have struggled with or that signifies something important to you, so that you can begin the journey to acceptance and celebration? Use your imagination and think about how you could use this sacred space to be true to your authentic self.

## EXPRESS YOUR DREAMS

Use the altar to enhance your dreams. Creating a manifestation board, wall or diary and placing this on your altar is a perfect way to do this. You can take clippings, print pictures, write quotes and draw images of anything that you'd like to manifest. You can split your manifestations into sections too. For example, I divided my manifestation board into career goals, personal goals, spirituality, love and self-expression, etc. This allows me to keep my journal in a more general and accessible form. However you choose to use your altar, adding a specific manifestation element can effectively further your inner trust.

## GET CREATIVE

Including personal artwork, clay sculptures or handmade items can also pay tribute to yourself and your capabilities. Designing your altar to suit you is also a wonderful way of reflecting your interests. If you like a minimal altar, honour that. If you love flowers, colour and maximalism, celebrate that! Whatever makes you feel like *you* – go with those natural impulses.

## SETTING THE TONE

Find scents that you love to burn, crystals that give you the best energy, and as many flowers and herbs as you like, to set the tone for your altar. If you'd like to create a specific feeling – for example, a self-love tone – burn scents such as rose, vanilla or honey. Flowers or dried flowers can also be the perfect way to celebrate yourself! Buying or picking your own flowers regularly is a beautiful, self-honouring ritual in itself. I learnt a long time ago that you don't need to wait for anyone else to buy you flowers!

## ADD TO IT REGULARLY

If you are able to and you have the space, add to your altar regularly to keep it updated and continuously honouring *you*. Take things away if they represent past versions of yourself and your thoughts, instincts and values, and replace them with anything that feels more like you currently. If you receive a gift that feels as though it is right for your sacred space, or if you find a quote in a magazine that you like, cut it out and place it at your altar or on your manifestation board. Embrace the way that the wants and needs of human beings change – and include an offering for yourself when you celebrate the Sabbats too! Make your altar more personal than it ever has been before.

When created with a pure heart and the right intentions, your self-love altar can enhance your connection with Wicca. Another way to nurture your relationship with yourself and the craft is through studying the Wiccan Rede, which we will be looking at next.

# 12.

# Living by the Rede

The Wiccan Rede is an amazing piece of sacred poetry that describes how Wiccans live and their belief system. The original author remains unknown. In 2020, when I started to re-evaluate my approach to Wicca, I reread the Rede frequently in order to understand its philosophy and what it could teach me. After looking deeper into the messages, I realised that I could learn so much from it about living every day in the modern world.

Crazily enough, I feel as if now, more than ever, the teachings within the Rede are more relevant to our lives. I think that we are gradually becoming further removed from trusting our intuition, surrounded by extreme or damaging influences, and potentially floating into a world led by a greedy minority. It's difficult not to engage with this way of thinking. The media and advertising constantly convey the message that incessant productivity, achievement and acquiring more things by spending more money is the only way to contentment and happiness.

Witchcraft can be viewed as a path towards freedom, away from the entrapping environment that we live in. Just deciding to partake in witchcraft is a sign of self-love to begin with. You are electing to enter an ethos in which you have choices and can make effective change. There is more to learn than the simple 'do what I say and you will be happy' philosophy that we are fed in everyday life. We can rediscover beauty. We can learn acceptance in ourselves and others. We can make change and live authentically without constantly doubting our worth, while also being a part of society. We can experience, beautifully, this incarnation. A great place to start within Wicca, before jumping into learning about the many different aspects of magick that you can participate in, is looking into the very human messages within this text. There are many different versions of the Wiccan Rede in which the wording differs slightly, but they all carry the same messages. I have taken a few phrases from it and broken down how I interpret them and what they mean to me. Please feel free to understand the words in whatever way makes sense to you.

## THE WICCAN REDE

*Bide the Wiccan Laws we must in Perfect Love and*
    *Perfect Trust.*
*Live and let live. Fairly take and fairly give.*
*Cast the Circle thrice about to keep the evil spirits out.*
*To bind the spell every time let the spell be spake in rhyme.*
*Soft of eye and light of touch, speak little, listen much.*
*Deosil go by the waxing moon, chanting out the Witches'*
    *Rune.*
*Widdershins go by the waning moon, chanting out the*
    *baneful rune.*
*When the Lady's moon is new, kiss the hand to Her, times two.*
*When the moon rides at her peak, then your heart's desire*
    *seek.*
*Heed the North wind's mighty gale, lock the door and drop*
    *the sail.*

*When the wind comes from the South, love will kiss thee on
the mouth.*
*When the wind blows from the West, departed souls will
have no rest.*
*When the wind blows from the East, expect the new and set
the feast.*
*Nine woods in the cauldron go, burn them fast and burn
them slow.*
*Elder be the Lady's tree, burn it not or cursed you'll be.*
*When the Wheel begins to turn, let the Beltane fires burn.*
*When the Wheel has turned to Yule, light the log and
the Horned One rules.*
*Heed ye flower, Bush and Tree, by the Lady, blessed be.*
*Where the rippling waters go, cast a stone and truth
you'll know.*
*When ye have a true need, harken not to others' greed.*
*With a fool no season spend, lest ye be counted as his friend.*
*Merry meet and merry part, bright the cheeks and warm
the heart.*
*Mind the Threefold Law you should, three times bad and
three times good.*
*When misfortune is enow, wear the blue star on thy brow.*
*True in love ever be, lest thy lover's false to thee.*
*Eight words the Wiccan Rede fulfil: An ye harm none,
do what ye will.*


## 'FAIRLY TAKE AND FAIRLY GIVE'

This phrase may seem straightforward, but worth mentioning
nonetheless as I think that finding balance wherever you can
is crucial to happiness; without it, we become filled with illu-
sion, bad karma or unbalanced energy. There are points within
life when you need to give and situations when you need to
take; but be sure that you're not taking more than giving. And
if you come to the conclusion that you are, look for ways to

give back, to volunteer and offer friendship where you can and assistance where it is needed.

I also relate this phrase to the concept of *samsara*, which is the Buddhist belief in the perpetual cycle of existence and dissatisfaction. Contradictory to some self-help advice, getting everything that we want in life might not be the best outcome. This doesn't mean remaining in a friendship or career that causes us harm or not striving for our authentic goals. It simply means to think about our wants and the reasons behind them. For example, sometimes we yearn for something that isn't good for us, such as a toxic relationship that, deep down, we know leaves us feeling devalued. We need to avoid the perpetual cycle of wanting or longing for something unachievable or something that we might have built a deceptive, distracting or potentially harmful fantasy around, and move on to focusing on making our reality more positive.

## 'SPEAK LITTLE, LISTEN MUCH'

This phrase in the Rede might not immediately jump out to you as being about self-love, but there is great wisdom found in those that have the ability to listen. Listening teaches patience and the importance of leaving our minds open to change. To me, this also relates to meditation, mindfulness and learning from every situation. As humans, we often see ourselves as superior to the natural world and sometimes as better than other people. We create hierarchy in our society so some can have more and feel that they have a higher value, which naturally leads to others having less and being made to feel less.

To retain an open mind, we must be available to listen and allow ourselves to be open to approaching every subject as a beginner, even those that we think we know well. So often, within the modern, western world, we are hell-bent on being right, expressing our opinions openly and loudly, and wanting to share everything that we do. Although that isn't always a bad thing! It encourages self-expression and community. But there is beauty, humility and liberation from angst in standing still or stepping back and being open to learning from everything around you.

## 'HARKEN NOT TO OTHERS' GREED'

This sentence fragment right here is the golden phrase for me. Whether we like to admit it or not, it's easy to become greedy. We are often subconsciously told that we are nothing without the fulfilment of materialistic (or 'worthy') achievement. We can become envious, comparing or fearful of our neighbours, thus avoiding genuine social contact. But what is success without love and others to share it? Everything we need to be happy is within us. Love is within us, and self-fulfilment can only come from within. You can search your whole life for contentment from careers, possessions and your bank balance, but there is no need, as you can discover it for free with some inner work and healing.

I also believe that this phrase relates to not being influenced by, or reactive to, the greed of others. Greed can typically make people unaware of their actions, and how those actions affect those around them; it's all-consuming, which is why it's such a powerful trait. You may suffer from the greed of others, we all do, but we don't have to let it control us or let it take away from the beauty we can find beyond materialism, craving and distress.

## 'WITH A FOOL NO SEASON SPEND'

To me, this phrase in the Wiccan Rede relates to relationships and self-growth. We must look out for whether other people are draining our energy or taking more than they give. I don't believe in a cut-throat existence of discarding relationships when something minor goes wrong. Still, I do believe in encouraging open communication. If the response to boundaries and genuine discussion is negative, it might be time to re evaluate the relationship and its foundations. Any friendship that has included early, authentic communication about boundaries, has been much healthier and is more likely to be present in my life a few years down the line. It is essential to check how you feel and listen to your intuition regarding whether relationships are hurting you in some way. Life is too short to live in fear of losing draining friendships. It's worth trying to use honesty to help repair a relationship or possibly collapse a bad one, ultimately freeing you both.

I also feel this phrase relates to lying to yourself or 'living as a fool'. We often unintentionally lie to ourselves about things, for example by blaming others for our problems, or we carry a false, negative self-image. This way of thinking can lead to living in unhappiness for years. The Wiccan lifestyle and teachings can help us by using practices such as divination, meditation or journaling, which strengthen our inner voices, enabling us to dispel any fake inner narratives that we are repeating. This concept also includes telling the truth to others, making choices that don't always make people happy, and learning to be unapologetically authentic, despite the possibility of offending those around us. Minimising or hiding our beliefs for the benefit of others will never result in happiness. Freeing ourselves of this habit can help with many different forms of intuitive work.

## 'MIND THE THREEFOLD LAW YOU SHOULD, THREE TIMES BAD AND THREE TIMES GOOD'

The Threefold Law is a concept within Wicca that is similar to karma. It teaches us that whatever we give out, we receive back three times over. This belief is not a command, but an encouragement to learn, heal, accept suffering and accept love. When you take notice of how you treat others around you and are mindful of the energy that you put out, regardless of where it's directed, you feel the weight of it. You carry that energy around with you, whether you are conscious of it or not. If you mistreat others and take from them constantly, you will suffer and have unresolved emotional pain. You are also being unkind to yourself through this. If you treat everything with disdain, you carry that contempt on your own shoulders. If you treat everything with loving awareness, it will be returned to you.

This concept doesn't teach us to feel the need to be perfect, but the need to be aware of our actions and the ripples of effect that they have on others. We often make up justifications for our actions, but these might need to be meditated on and stripped back. Typically, if your intentions are good, the results rarely come back to bite you.

## 'EIGHT WORDS THE WICCAN REDE FULFIL: AN YE HARM NONE, DO WHAT YE WILL'

Finally, although it comes at the end, this phrase lies at the heart of the Rede. As I mentioned earlier, in my initial days of Wicca, I became obsessed with people-pleasing as a way of trying to live up to these words. Unfortunately, I still had many issues with relationships over those years, and some led to me being in traumatising scenarios. Not everyone has our best interests at heart and it's important to use our intuition while navigating whether it's worth putting emotional effort into those who are draining us. I still believe kindness and gratitude to others are essential – but you also need to give yourself the utmost compassion and acceptance. Without self-love and tolerance, you will still find strife within your relationships and interactions with other people.

We often live with hidden exceptions that we permit in others' behaviour or subconsciously allow everyone that we meet to treat us exactly how they want to. With boundaries in place, we will be surrounded by deeper love and healthier relationships. 'Harming none' includes yourself. So, if you're looking to live a happier life, I would start with self-forgiveness and self-acceptance before all, focus on your boundaries, morals and where you find joy, then align your life to match up with your truths – and see where it takes you.

# 13.

# Healing and Letting Go

Before I came back to Wicca, I had convinced myself that I was on a set path, with no awareness that I could take a different route at any time. I honestly believed that the things that were actually important to my soul and heart were unnecessary and insignificant in the greater scheme of things. But when I started meditating, as my world opened up I began to connect the dots and realised that I treated myself disrespectfully most of the time. I would notice myself subconsciously repeating 'you're such an idiot' to myself several times a day, along with 'you're fat, you're ugly, you've messed your life up beyond repair', etc. I would shy away from the mirror, and when I did catch a glimpse of myself, I couldn't appreciate what I saw.

I had a history of blaming myself for the trauma that I had faced and, in the past, had punished myself physically. I started to realise that the way that I spoke to myself had a powerful effect on my confidence and self-value, and it also affected those around me. I became very aware that changes were essential in order to make my life feel worth living.

I decided that I needed to take steps towards being kinder to myself and to gain control over my feelings of self-hatred. I knew that the first step was simple and that my life would not improve if I didn't truly think that I deserved better. I chose to take what I had learnt from Wicca and use it to help me to accept, honour and connect with myself again. Increasing self-love is fundamental to understanding the potential that is within all of us to create a well-lived, joyful life. We often tend to forget that we are meant to enjoy living. Why do you think Wiccans celebrate the earth eight times a year? Because we know that life is not meant to be a drudge of relentless work, coping and unhappiness. We are supposed to marvel in the gift of life.

## THE POWER OF EMOTION

As humans, we experience a wide spectrum of emotions, sometimes several at once, and not one of them is a 'bad' emotion. We can learn something about ourselves from each of these feelings. The issue that we sometimes find is that we create a story behind the emotion, making it feel as though we *are* that emotion. So we carry it, we keep it in, and sometimes we revisit the story over and over again, unable to let it go, when in reality these feelings pass and are simply our bodies trying to tell us something about ourselves, our actions and our lives.

For example, if we feel guilt, this might be telling us that we don't want to repeat an action, and shame can indicate that there might be something we are doing that we need to explore further, possibly in order to change a pattern and recover from it. Anger can tell us many things; maybe we need to protect ourselves or that we have left something unresolved in our subconscious? Sorrow is telling us to grieve and release, (crying is part of the healing process) and joy reminds us of the beauty in the world. The important thing is, those emotions should *not* be contained within us. If unreleased or unexplored, they will build up throughout the body's energy centres and prevent us from living as our true, authentic selves. I've mentioned the chakra system earlier in this book; if any of our chakra energy centres become blocked through lack of expression, this can also cause physical and emotional issues. To unblock them, we must find a way to let these feelings out into the universe instead of allowing them to build up and take control of us.

## WHAT WICCA TEACHES US ABOUT HEALING AND LETTING GO

When I returned to Wicca, I felt like a door to another world had been opened, and I could see and think clearly for the first time in years. I learnt that life would go on despite my past and how badly I had treated myself. I didn't have to hate myself, misuse others, work in a job that I despised, or date people who were mean to me. I learnt that the world would keep turning, and I could change who I was – not necessarily my outward appearance, but my thoughts.

Wicca teaches us this through encouragement of love for the earth and its natural cycles. We do not choose the seasons, nor when the sun rises and falls, and we don't have to understand Mother Nature, but we have the opportunity to work alongside her and to make life better. We cannot control everything, nor are we above anything, but we can always make the best of what we have. We can continually improve on elements of our lives that are not making us happy.

Hearing hope beyond the mundane 'live because you have to' narrative that I heard from others, felt beautiful. There was life beyond my perception, and there was even life inside of me as yet undiscovered. I decided that everything I had experienced wasn't going to define who I am, and I could take steps towards a more positive reality. I really felt as though I was beginning to heal.

I began connecting to my spirit, and rediscovering ideas in

Wiccan teachings that had helped me so much in my teens, but that I had forgotten. I learnt once again about honouring the feminine divine inside of me, finding joy in the present, connecting to my true nature, and helping me balance my ego. I discovered that the person that I had spent years believing was me, wasn't me at all. I was dying and being reborn again. My mind was connecting to my spirit, and my soul was catching up with me. This new mindset pushed me to forget about the complications of who we are told we need to be and to turn towards the truth of existence and purpose, which is to survive, to be, and to accept.

## LETTING GO OF PAST VERSIONS OF YOURSELF SPELL

For a long time, I struggled to let go of phases of my life, or past versions of myself, due to trauma attachments and finding comfort in being unhappy. This might have been because unresolved emotions kept drawing me back in or because it was easier to fall back on old feelings than to move on. When we forgive, accept and learn to understand our past selves we allow a new version of ourselves to flourish and grow, without letting old emotions that no longer serve us hold us back.

This spell focuses on letting the universe take this off our hands, using some simple candle and moon magick. The three black candles within this spell help let go of any negativity you may be holding on to and the purple candle helps to break habits. You will find the best results around the time of the full moon!

**Intent:** To let go of a past version of yourself or a time in your life you cling on to.

Perfect time: Sunday evening, or for best results, the day before a full moon.

You will need:

a picture of yourself from the past (*representing the time of your life that you're struggling to release*)
3 black candles
1 purple candle

* Before you begin the ritual, be sure to clear anything that's triggering you out of your space or daily life for the magick to have its full effect! You can't let go when you're constantly being put back into a difficult place.

* When you are ready, take your picture and place it in the centre of a table or work area, position the 3 black candles around it and the purple one nearest to you.

* Before you light the candles, spend 3 minutes meditating on why you need to forgive and let go of this past version of yourself, whether there is guilt, nostalgia, want or any cycles of pain associated with it.

* Once you have done this, light the black candles and then the purple candle.

* With your index finger on your more dominant hand, carefully draw 3 circles clockwise in the air well above the candles, activating this intention. Then say these words out loud:

> *I release the old me*
> *and free the present me,*
> *letting go of my past*
> *to move forward at last.*

* Once you have finished doing this, blow out the candles in a clockwise direction, then put the picture out of sight or dispose of it as you wish.

# IDEAS ABOUT LIFE AFTER DEATH

Diving further into Wiccan concepts, I began to acknowledge the conversations in Wicca about letting go and also death. A few years ago, I read about the ideas of Summerland – the realm of the afterlife – and the exploration of Wiccan beliefs about life after death. Some of this is close to the Buddhist beliefs on this subject. So, what does happen when we die?

My personal belief is that we leave our bodies and disperse into the universe. We become colour, the walls, the ceilings, the roofs, the trees, the clouds, the blue in the sky, then the stars; and we are nothing, but we are everything. This belief, to me, leads me back to the foundation of why I love Wicca so much. I believe in nature, the earth, the sky, the sun, and the moon; everything we need to learn from sits around us daily, and we are home when we know this truth. We die daily and are reborn every second.

It may take work, but you can find peace, love and live happily as a part of the earth. After listening to different witches speak on the matter, it makes sense to me that we come into this world and go out of it the same way. We are nature. We have some of the same DNA as stars, trees, and fungi, so I believe, like nature, letting go entirely means letting go of the idea that we have to be anything other than human. In this way, we free ourselves to live and exist in our own authentic ways, which will bring us true joy instead of permanent wanting and dissatisfaction.

# CAN WITCHCRAFT HEAL TRAUMA?

I am not a trained therapist, nor do I have any professional experience in trauma, but I do feel that witchcraft and spiritual assistance can help to heal suffering and distress. However, I don't believe that these things can *cure* trauma for you. I personally have experienced a great amount of help from spirituality, sobriety, therapy and meditation.

Trauma can be collective and stem from many minor circumstances throughout your life or from a single significant, painful event. Shock and distress sticks in our physical bodies and our subconscious, and comes out in so many ways. So, it makes sense to me that by experiencing energy healing through spellcraft, we can help push some of those damaging feelings from our bodies or transfer the power into something more helpful. However, I believe that the only way to fully work through trauma is through personal inner work, combined with therapy. Wiccan practices can help you with the internal change, but please seek help if you are struggling.

# Part 4
## Magick for the World

# 14.

# Manifesting for a Better Reality

Escapism is often tempting and can be a coping strategy for stressful times, but personally, I feel that it is essential to try to live in the real world and to learn to cope with the daily issues that can have a detrimental effect on our contentment. Otherwise, we may turn around and realise that by avoiding the problems that make our realities difficult to deal with, we've unintentionally made our lives feel flat.

I think that, initially, it is crucial to put some thought into and identify what you are dealing with and what is weighing you down. A great place to start is to perform the ritual and journaling prompts that will help you to get to know yourself in Chapter 1, pages 4–8. Also, journaling and building inner trust can help you to identify any problems, habits or situations that you want to change, or if you feel that something is missing from your life and you want to attract this to you.

Manifestation is a potent tool that really works. Ever since I was a child, I've been using it. My mum used to tell me that she would go outside into the garden in the dark and ask the stars for things that she needed. So I started to copy her and do the same. I only did this when I felt that I really needed to, and the universe always came back to me!

Yet we have to accept that we can't manifest against the universe; we have to work with it. We are unable to manifest away pain or suffering, as they are natural elements of our experience and the world is doing its own thing. However, we can be specific and work alongside the universe by showing it that we are ready for whatever we're asking of it. And if we're not prepared for the outcome, the universe won't give it to us yet; it's that simple.

Manifestation also requires high energy, so you can't sit around and wait for things to happen. You have to want whatever you request with all of your soul; thus it's already yours in some way. For manifestation to work, you need to be realistic, proactive and practical. Get some paper and a pencil, time it right, create plans and make sure that, after putting your manifestations out there, you take any relevant opportunities that come your way. The trick is to write and think as though whatever you are asking for is already yours. And then show the universe gratitude.

Here's an example:

- *Don't write:* 'Soon, I will pass my driving test.'
- *Do write:* 'I will have passed my driving test by 18 September.'

Be precise, so that the universe understands that the intended outcome is meant for you individually!

## THREE BASIC MANIFESTATION PRACTICES

If you've never tried manifestation before, start with these three techniques. The more you practise, the more powerful the results! (It is a good idea to keep a journal specifically for writing down your manifestations.)

## REPETITION MANIFESTATION

This technique is excellent for a singular, specific manifestation and can be used for any purpose.

**Perfect time:** Anytime.

**You will need:**

a journal and a pen

* First, grab your journal and write your manifestation. For example, 'I'm so grateful that I will get a promotion at work by the end of the year.' You have to know in your soul that it's yours!

* Now repeat the manifestation on every line of the entire page, except on the last line.

* On the last line, write: 'Thank you for blessing me with this universal gift', or another expression of gratitude that feels right to you.

* If you sense that this manifestation needs a boost, repeat it in the mirror first thing in the morning, as often and as many times as you like!

## PRAYER MANIFESTATION

This technique is super simple and can be used for daily manifestations that need to be quickly achieved. For example, if you have a job interview or need extra luck for the day, you can use this at short notice.

**Perfect time:** Any morning.

**You will need:**

a mirror
1 white candle
pen and paper (*optional*)

✶ Start by standing in front of your mirror and light your candle. Then, take a few deep breaths and read your prayer out loud, repeating it three times. You can write your prayer down if you need to.

✶ This is my prayer, but feel free to use this as a template and create your own:

> *Today will be filled with joy and contentment.*
> *Today I will achieve (insert your requirement).*
> *I need this because (insert your reasons).*
> *Now I thank the universe for providing me with this*
> *energy.*

Blow out the candle and bring this uplifting energy with you throughout the day!

## SEVEN-DAY MANIFESTATIONS

This method can be used for any manifestation that you want to achieve after a period of seven days.

**Perfect time:** Begin on a Sunday evening and repeat until the following Sunday for the best results.

**You will need:**

paper and a pen
a small bag or purse to keep your paper in

★ Write an affirmation or a manifestation on your piece of paper, fold it up and carry it around with you for seven days. An affirmation is an expression of what you know to be true, while a manifestation is about welcoming in something from the universe. Whichever you choose, you can place it in your pocket, your bag, or your purse. Just make sure it is somewhere safe so that you won't lose it!

★ Before you sleep at night, read your manifestation out loud and then place it under your pillow.

★ Remove the note from under your pillow the next morning and repeat.

## IS MANIFESTING DIFFERENT FROM SPELLCASTING?

Though there are differing opinions on this subject, to me, manifesting is magick, the same as any other form of spellcasting. Its foundation still lies in setting the intention. However, because of societal preconceptions, some people are still scared of or misinformed about the word 'witchcraft'. They might prefer to use the term 'manifestation' as it has lighter, more generally accepted connotations.

I like to use spellwork and prepare more intricate rituals for subjects that I need a greater focus on. This is why I mainly tend to use manifesting at the full or new moon, maybe if I am not feeling so strong, or if I don't want to cast a spell or perform a moon-related ritual for some reason. As usual, intuition informs my decision over this.

All in all, manifesting is definitely worth doing. It's efficient too! Use it alongside your craft for creating effective change with some writing magick, and help to manifest a better reality!

# 15.

# Protection

As much as we may wish to manifest a better reality and make the world a more harmonious place, there may be times when we find ourselves faced by forces or individuals that don't always have our best interests at heart. Protecting yourself with witchcraft is a powerful way to safeguard your energy generally, during a ritual, or from any negativity that may come your way.

If you are looking to shield yourself during magick, always cast a circle (see page 39)! But there is also a benefit in incorporating defensive energy into your home and your daily routine. We often overlook the extent to which our spaces hold energy and how this built-up negativity can affect our moods and wellbeing.

Protecting yourself can be tricky at times, so let's start with the basic concept of emotional and self-protection. First of all, be aware that regularly entering compromising scenarios that leave you feeling the size of a mouse will drain you more quickly than an iPhone battery. Second, if you're not taking care of yourself physically and are always ignoring your intuition, this will exhaust you too. Either way, any habits that make you feel bad about yourself or devalued need to be re-evaluated and changed if possible.

Also, of course, if you are feeling unhappy a lot of the

time, this could indicate that you need to do some inner work and create daily rituals that will help you to check in with your emotions, look after your mental health and be mindful of your lifestyle. If you have medication, remember to take it. If meditation helps you, practise that regularly. If working out creates inner balanced energy for you, try to prioritise time for that! There's no point protecting yourself with spiritual influences if you are not doing what you can in your life generally to maintain inner peace.

## SIMPLE AIDS FOR DAILY PROTECTION

There are some easy steps that you can take to give yourself a little extra magickal protection. These include:

**Shielding crystals** such as quartz, obsidian, black tourmaline, agate and carnelian are all great for this purpose, especially when worn.

**Wearing protective witchcraft symbols** such as the pentagram, triquetra (the Triple Goddess symbol), or an elemental symbol.

**Dressing in colours such as green, yellow, red, or pink** when you're out and about will help defend you from harm.

**Raising your energy levels** by engaging in anything that you know will bring you joy or serve your long-term goals or needs (may be obvious – but super important).

**Prioritising** and avoiding using elsewhere the energy you need for essential elements of your own life.

## WILD GARLIC PESTO FOR PROTECTION

Certain foods can also aid in psychic shielding, especially if you're looking for something quick to incorporate into your day! Many fresh herbs can aid your defences, but my all-time favourite is wild garlic. This spell is used for protection during spiritual practices, spellwork or at any time when you feel that you need additional shielding.

Wild garlic tends to be ready to harvest around April to May and has green leaves and star-shaped white flowers. To identify wild garlic, rub your hands on the plant and smell them – they have a faint, fresh scent, somewhere between garlic and chives. It is **really, really important to be certain** that you have picked wild garlic, as it looks very similar to some poisonous plants. If in doubt, buy some from your local market instead.

Use of a sigil and the clockwise movement during this spell helps to activate the protective intention. If you wish to work other kinds of magick, you can substitute the wild garlic with parsley (for passion and fertility) or basil (for good fortune).

**Intent:** To aid in protection.

**Perfect time:** When wild garlic is in season in the spring.

**You will need:**

100g (3½oz) wild garlic leaves
70g (2½oz) pine nuts
salt and pepper to taste
1 to 3 tsp Italian herbs (*such as basil*)
juice of 1 lemon
4 tsp nutritional yeast
chilli flakes to taste

*Optional extras*:

a jar or two with lids
paint
kitchen witchery spoon or wand

✴ Forage or shop for some wild garlic. Take your wild garlic home and rinse it gently.

✴ Start making your pesto by briefly toasting the pine nuts in a pan at low heat until they're golden brown. Allow them to cool.

✴ Add the pine nuts, wild garlic, salt, pepper, herbs, lemon juice, yeast and chili flakes to a blender and pulse until it creates a textured pesto.

* Place in your jar and close the lid.

* Paint this sigil on top of the jar in black paint:

This translates roughly as: 'I am emotionally and spiritually protected from any negative energy that may come my way.'

* Take your wand or index finger and draw three circles clockwise around the rim of the jar, helping activate the protective element of the spell and seal the sigil.

* Use immediately with a dish of your choosing (pasta or pesto garlic bread are my personal recommendations), or store in the fridge for up to 3 days.

## PROTECTING YOUR SPACE

Protecting your space is simple, and there are a couple of rules that I like to follow to save energy:

* Never let overly negative people invade your space (if you can help it). If they do, cleanse ASAP!
* Keep up the vibrations in your home! Decorate and create energy in your house that makes you feel comfortable and happy.
* Cleanse your home regularly! The next chapter will cover cleansing and its importance in protecting a home, but yes, cleanse!

Here are a few more suggestions to help you make your home a safe and happy place.

# SYMBOLS

Using sigils or symbolism in your home is an excellent way of actually casting a spell to protect your space. You can draw sigils into pictures or draw a sign onto some paper and stick it near your front entrance, or you can use your fingers to trace them onto doors.

---

## PRACTICAL MAGICK TIP – USE A PROTECTIVE MIST

Mix a few essential oils with protective properties (I recommend basil or rosemary for a light, fresh scent) and some moon water in a spray bottle. Charge this overnight with a crystal placed on it – jade, amethyst quartz and tourmaline are great for this purpose – and spray it onto a door that it won't damage. You can draw a sigil into the damp area! Or use it occasionally as a protective spray.

---

## COLOUR AND ART

Red, pink, green and yellow can also be used to ward off negative energy and protect your environment. Hanging up pictures, painting walls and having furniture which incorporate these colours is a fairly effortless way to include a bit of extra defensive energy in your home.

Speaking of colour, making use of these hues in art can be applied for protection too! You can create paintings, drawings, textiles and 3D art with a defensive intent behind it, or you can use an image of something that communicates protection and vigour to you. You can also use pictures of deities that enable you to feel safeguarded, inspire vibrant energy, or anything that symbolises strength.

# NATURE

As obvious as it may sound, when looking to protect yourself and your home, and any witchcraft you do, you can turn to nature for help. There are so many different plants, herbs, trees and crystals that can assist in safeguarding your space. (My personal favourites are the crystal malachite, and the plants aloe vera, mint and the Chinese money plant.) You can hang them up, plant them and place them around you to help with the energy in your home. You can also create wall hangings, pictures, and chimes to ward off negative energy. Traditionally, wooden chimes would have been hung outside our houses to scare away negative spirits.

## WOODEN HANGING TO WARD AWAY NEGATIVE ENERGY

This hanging protects your environment from potentially harmful energy and also allows any negativity to be visible to you when it enters your home. Use your intuition if you instantly feel uncomfortable with someone who is present in your house, they may be an energy vampire. The shape of this hanging represents an air symbol to work with the elements and to create positive energy with the air passing through it!

**Intent:** To protect your home.

**Perfect time:** Best made on a Saturday.

**You will need:**

3 similar sized sticks
2 small hag stones and 1 slightly bigger hag stone (*a pebble with a hole through it, often found on beaches*)
sturdy string or yarn

white paint and a small paintbrush
cleansing incense such as sage or nag champa

★ Start by going for a walk, taking some time to find some hag stones and sticks that feel right for the job! Try to find sturdy sticks about 20cm (8in) long. Ensure that your stones and sticks are completely dry before using them.

★ Arrange the three sticks in a triangle shape for this hanging.

★ Tie the string around where two sticks overlap to hold them together, then loop it around the stick until it reaches where the next pair of stick ends overlap. Repeat until you have a fastened triangle.

★ Take your largest stone and, in white paint, paint this specific sigil on it, which roughly translates as: 'Negativity, stay away from this home':

Allow this to dry.

★ Take 60cm (24in) of yarn and loop it through your largest hag stone. Tie the yarn together at the top of the hag stone to secure it.

★ To fasten the stone to your wooden triangle, simply tie a knot at the top of the yarn that's attached to the stone, leaving enough space for you to tie it again around the centre of the stick that acts as the base of the triangle.

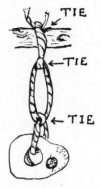

*How to tie each stone.*

✷ With your two smaller hag stones, follow the same routine to fasten them to your sticks, but place them on either side of your larger stone. You can paint whatever you'd like on these stones and paint the sticks too if you wish!

*The finished hanging.*

✷ Lastly, tie some string around the top of the point of the stick triangle, creating a loop so you can hang it up.

* Place your hanging inside or out. Once it's hung up, cleanse it with your incense, circling the hanging a few times with the smoke to activate it and the sigil. The sigil may wash off if you hang it where it's exposed to rain, but it will still be effective!

# 16.

# Cleansing

An essential aspect of keeping your space sacred involves regularly cleansing it of negative energies. In addition to protecting your immediate environment, there will be times when you need to shift some energy out of there too. Whether we are aware of it or not, we carry energy within us and it is present in our surroundings. If we don't look after our minds, our energy centres become blocked, and the same goes for our homes. So regular cleansing helps to create and maintain a loving environment that we are more likely to thrive in, and it can change how we live and feel every day.

## A WITCH'S CLEANING GUIDE

Cleaning may or may not be something that we like to do, but if we incorporate witchcraft into the mix, this will help lift our energy a little too! I try to give my house a thorough clean at least once a week and a quick clean every day. This might seem excessive or unnecessary, depending on what kind of personality you have. For me, this amount of cleaning is *a lot*, as I'm a naturally messy person. However, after learning about the energy that all items carry, the Wiccan lifestyle has been the only thing that's genuinely motivated me to clean. If you've had a difficult or low week, your house needs to be cleared of this. Here are some simple things to do:

**Banish negative energy.** When you are cleaning, brush down an area with either your hands or by vacuuming around the room, and say the words, 'I free you from negative energy.'

**Dust regularly**, giving extra attention to areas of your home that might usually be neglected. Negative energy could be hiding in a dusty corner that you have ignored!

**Clean your altar every week.** This is your *most* sacred place where your magickal tools lay. Treat them like the special items that they are! Try to remove everything from your altar, then, dust, polish and clean every item before replacing it. Bless your altar by lighting some incense when everything is back in its place.

**Add magickally charged baking powder** to your household cleaning solutions. Baking powder in itself has some excellent cleansing properties. If you're thinking about ways to add a little bit of magick to your everyday cleaner; just try adding charged baking powder to it for a magickal boost.

**Regularly perform a spiritual cleanse** with herbs, incense, smoke of any kind, charged water, or a chime whenever the energy in your home feels heavy. Then, after you have done your weekly clean, perform a short cleansing ritual.

## WEEKLY CLEANSING RITUAL

Here is a ritual to help refresh any stagnant or negative energy
in your space! Prepare it at least a day in advance.

**Intent:** To clear away negative vibes.

**Perfect time:** Perfect on a Sunday after you have cleaned!

**You will need:**

a glass bottle with a top
1 stick of incense (*such as sage or violet, which assist in
    shielding an area*)
a lighter or matches
a few petals or flower heads (*I recommend lavender for peace
    and safety*)
moon water
a crystal
a small spray bottle (*optional*)

☆ Take your bottle and open the lid. Light your incense and
   place it into the bottle for a few seconds, filling the bottle
   with smoke.

* Then place your petals into the bottle and fill it with charged moon water.

* You can choose to place your crystal into the bottle if it will fit, or place it on top of the closed lid. Leave this for 24 hours on a windowsill or outside in full view of the moon.

* Pour the mixture into a spray bottle, filtering out the crystal and petals. Or you can place a small amount in a shallow bowl so that you can flick it over the area to be cleansed.

* Keep the water somewhere cool and use it when needed to banish negative energies.

## USING SOUND TO CLEANSE

Cleansing with sound is a very effective way to mix up the energy in your space, making it easier to ward off stagnant negativity. Using sound can be positive and calming; and purifying an area with sound can also be great for days when you're not feeling overly optimistic. In addition, this is a smoke-free method which might be more appropriate if you have pets, are pregnant, or have young children. You can use Tibetan bells, chimes, handheld bells, singing bowls, or even clapping or singing.

You could also try the following:

• Hang a bell near your front door. When you get in from a day out, ring the bell around you, in this way clearing the energy from you and leaving it at the door, along with anything emotionally draining from your day. (See also 'Cleansing Yourself', page 186.)

• After cleaning, walk around your house ringing a bell to get rid of the last of the negative energy that may be lingering.

# CLEANSING YOUR ENVIRONMENT OF HEAVY ENERGY

You might be struggling to cleanse your home because of something traumatic or emotionally demanding that has been happening in your space. In that case, you might need something more thorough than a simple cleansing ritual. You may need to completely change the room's vibe – to cleanse, clean and re-energise the space with all of the elements to move past whatever's been lingering there.

**Intent:** Clearing traumatic and challenging energy from a space.

**Perfect time:** Preferably a Sunday when you are feeling emotionally ready for this.

**You will need:**

sprigs of 3 different types of dried herb (*lavender, thyme and rosemary are excellent for cleansing, calming and clearing energy, and burn well*)
string
lighter or matches
non-flammable plate or tile
small amount of charged moon-water in a bowl
salt

★ Start this ritual by shifting around the furniture in the area that you'd like to cleanse. If any trauma has happened here or has any relation to this room, this step is particularly essential to lifting the pain and distress out of any objects that you own. Move your furniture around and almost try to create a new space within the old one.

* Clear things out, sort your cupboards and wardrobe, get some bags of unwanted items ready to take to charity shops, and dust the ceiling.

* When you feel content with your new space, create a herb stick with the dried herbs that you've accumulated, tying them together with the string at intervals along their length, so that you can burn them as one, and placing them to one side.

* Start this next part of the ritual by opening your windows, taking your moon water and sprinkling and flicking it around the room to begin the cleansing process. As you do this, say these words once:

> *I cleanse the energy from this room*
> *that weighs me down*
> *and brings me pain.*

* Use your intuition to decide when you have cleansed the room enough with this element.

* Then light your herb stick, but extinguish it almost immediately by pressing it onto a non-flammable plate or tile so that it is just smoking rather than burning.

* Now waft the smoking herb stick around the room carefully and repeat the verse above.

* Follow this by taking the salt and flicking a small amount of it around the room, repeating the verse once more.

* Afterwards, hold your hands on your chest so that you can feel your energy and love pass into them. Visualise your strength, power and your ability to move through anything.

* Go around the room and use your hands to brush away any remaining energy from your possessions and furniture, repeating the verse a last time.

* Stand in your room, hold your hands to your side and say the words:

> *I bless this room as a sanctuary*
> *for my soul,*
> *my heart*
> *and my mind.*
> *So mote it be.*

* Allow the room to clear and then shut the windows to signify the end of the ritual.

## CLEANSING YOURSELF

We carry most of our inner energy in centres throughout our body, known commonly as the chakras. Even though this is not a Wiccan concept, I've still found it helpful to learn from these traditions regarding emotional uncluttering. Here is a list of questions that I like to ask myself when I'm feeling blocked and need to do some inner reflection, and which you might find useful too.

Are you:

- surrounding yourself with positive people and letting go of friendships that aren't making you happy?
- finding the courage to change the facets of your life that make you miserable?
- finding acceptance of things that you cannot change through meditation, therapy and journaling? (This practice includes letting go of the constant feeling that we need to improve ourselves.)
- showing up as yourself authentically, even when it's difficult?
- allowing yourself the time to cry when you need to, and the time to nurture yourself?

- releasing all emotions healthily and beneficially instead of letting them build up?
- speaking your mind and always telling the truth, even if you need to be gentle about it?
- inadvertently welcoming sources of negativity into your life as forms of coping, such as social media, high media intake, excessive alcohol, drug consumption, binge eating, consuming large amounts of sugary food, or pushing those close to you away?

Once you've taken a look at your answers, you can begin to tackle any imbalances through daily emotional cleansing with the following steps.

## REGULAR MEDITATION

If I haven't already tooted the horn for meditation enough to convince you to do this regularly, here's my last shot. Daily meditation is the foundation for helping you to get on top of your energy, experiencing your emotions and feeling release when needed and having a calm and clear mind. When your energy is flying all over the place, you need to come back to yourself, so meditate, dammit, mediate!

## EATING WELL AND EXERCISE

This may or may not seem like a given to everyone, and please don't take this as an instruction to start working out and eating cleanly. However, getting out for regular walks, swimming, doing yoga and Pilates, and eating a good range of whole foods can boost your energy. Nutrition and exercise don't have to be the focus of your life. It is just a simple reminder that you can exercise when you feel like it and eat well to raise your energy a little!

## RAISING YOUR VIBRATIONS

This may go without saying, but you can do various things to grow your vibrations. You could carry around specific crystals such as aquamarine and lithium quartz; smoke cleanse yourself (by burning but then immediately extinguishing herbs before wafting them around yourself); light candles in your home; practise forms of divination, and regularly manifest. Journaling can also help. Documenting your emotions on a page and then keeping them held there can be highly therapeutic. You can also raise your vibrations with simple self-care! Give yourself time to recharge after a mentally exhausting day; a delicious bubble bath, a facemask, a scrumptious meal or dressing yourself in your favourite clothes can all help you feel your best and improve your vitality.

---

### HOW TO PERFORM A TRADITIONAL SMOKE CLEANSE

Light some incense or a dried herbs such as sage or a piece of sacred wood. Immediately extinguish the flame and waft the incense or herb etc. around the area with the intention of removing any negative or stagnant energy from the space.

---

## TRANSFORMATION CLEANSE

If you're looking for inner transformation and feel as though you need to cleanse yourself thoroughly, this ritual can assist you with creating internal change after a challenging or stagnant period of your life. As a Wiccan, I'm really into symbolism, so when I can feel myself entering a new phase of life, I like to do a ritual of some kind. Personally, it seems often to be either a new haircut, tattoo or a special ceremony just for me. This ritual might not be accessible to everyone. Still, it's certainly one to think about for anyone who loves a wild swim and feels the need for an entire body cleanse and an emotional uplift.

**Perfect time:** On the last day of a moon cycle.

You will need:

just yourself and somewhere you can wild swim (*e.g. river, pond, secluded beach*)
swimsuit or possibly a wet suit (*optional*)

* Start by taking yourself to a place where you can wild swim safely. It's nice to find somewhere where there won't be a lot of disturbance, but if it makes you feel more secure, go with one other person you trust. (For guidance on wild swimming safely, I'd recommend looking at wild swimming websites first.) You can do this swim sky-clad (i.e. naked) if you wish, but making sure you feel safe enough to do this is of utmost important. It is a personal choice, and I usually feel just as connected in a swimsuit.

* Immerse yourself in the water. As the water touches you, visualise it cleansing old energy away, blessing you with its natural flow. Get used to the water temperature and when you feel comfortable, lie back, float or rest your head in the water, or stand and float your upper body if the water is shallow.

* Visualise the old energy leaving you, drifting away with the water, leaving your body forever.

* After you've done this, imagine that there is a new light surrounding you, a warm, golden glow, creating beauty and love that encircles you, transforming you into a new radiance.

* Do this for a few minutes and then go for a swim and enjoy yourself or take yourself out of the water and dry off.

* You may want to do a manifestation this evening to help put your transformation into action (see the manifestation rituals in Chapter 14, page 166).

## DAILY CLEANSING

As with all witchcraft, cleansing can be welcomed as a part of your regular routine. You can, of course, opt for a traditional daily smoke cleanse if you feel the need, but if you don't have the time, try one of these for a quick and effective lift!

Here are my top three daily cleansing rituals.

## MORNING CLEANSE

This coffee ritual is a simple inner-cleansing spell for the mornings. I typically use this super easy spell when I'd like to reset my body and cleanse it of negativity.

During this ritual, we will be using coffee and some herbs; mint seems to work well. Mint is not only superb for digestion, aiding anxiety and reducing nausea, but magickally, it's excellent for protection, healing and banishing negative energy. Depending on the herb that you would like to use, its spiritual properties and the results that you would like to achieve, you can replace mint with something else.

Coffee is also great for grounding, boosting power and overcoming emotional blockages. You can also stick with decaf if you have issues with anxiety or would rather not drink caffeinated coffee.

**Intent:** Resetting and cleansing yourself of negativity.

**Perfect time:** Any morning that you feel the need to press the reset button.

**You will need:**

a cup of coffee (*fresh, ethically sourced and brewed in a V60 or cafetière is preferable, but instant is fine too, so please use whatever works for you!*)
a few sprigs of fresh or dried mint
a kitchen witchery spoon (*optional*)

✶ Boil your kettle, make your coffee and find a comfortable seat.

✶ Take the spoon and stir your coffee three times clockwise. While you do this, say the words:

> *Cleanse my body and mind of negative energy.*

Simple!

✶ Place your mint in the coffee, take a seat and sip slowly. Enjoy it and be present while you drink, notice the tastes and scents as you do this, and enjoy a balanced day!

## EVENING CLEANSE FOR A RESTFUL SLEEP

Whenever I have an overwhelming day or a busy mind, I find myself having either an unrestful sleep or find myself in negative dream states. Sleep helps me think straight, keeps up my energy and raises my vibrations. Performing this cleansing ritual can ensure you're not carrying any overwhelming energy within the area where you sleep or within yourself.

**Intent:** Clearing negative energy before bedtime.

**Perfect time:** Before bed when you're feeling overwhelmed or restless.

**You will need:**

moon water
salt

★ Pour a small amount of moon water into a small bowl, followed by three pinches of salt.

★ Dip your fingers into the bottom of the bowl and sprinkle it around your room. While you're doing this, say the words:

*Banish negativity and stress from this space and allow me to rest!*

★ Follow this by sprinkling some of the water around yourself. As you're doing this, say the words:

*Banish negativity and stress from this body, and allow it to rest!*

★ Place the bowl down and enjoy your restful sleep.

## ANTI-ANXIETY TEA SPELL

This simple anti-anxiety remedy uses numbers and herbal magick to help calm your nerves for twenty-four hours. Honey and agave both have beneficial properties as healing syrups, helping to soothe the stomach and aid digestion. Agave is an alternative to honey to allow for those with dietary preferences. If using honey, I suggest sourcing it from a local beekeeper, as fresh local honey has more substantial healing effects. However, this spell is not a cure but a calming, helping hand. Chamomile is an antioxidant with properties that naturally calm your nervous system. Use this up to 3 times a week and enjoy the natural effects of magickal chamomile!

**Intent:** To help soothe anxiety.

Perfect time: Any morning.

You will need:

3 to 4 tsp fresh chamomile
boiling water
1 tsp honey or agave syrup

*Optional extras:*
If you have a preferred cup or kitchen witchery spoon that
   you like to use, use these now!

✳ Put the chamomile in the mug and add boiled water.

✳ Slowly and carefully, circle around the rim of the mug with
   your index finger 24 times, each time saying the words: *'Anxiety away!'*

✳ Add the honey or agave syrup to your drink and stir three
   times to activate and seal the spell.

✳ Drink the mixture, and allow yourself to be completely present while consuming it, with no distractions! Enjoy its
   calming effects for 24 hours.

# 17.

# Physical Self-expression and Connection

Physical self-expression can be a powerful way of communicating and releasing our feelings, thoughts and needs. Placing our inward emotions out into the world is so beneficial for our wellbeing; and we can use our bodies as a canvas for this purpose. The phrase 'your body is an altar' is one that I like to live by. Ever since I can remember, I've taken pleasure in adorning myself with clothes, accessories, symbolic jewellery and tattoos that reflect periods of my life, my spirituality and my creativity. Unfortunately, some parts of society, the media and advertising often lead us to think that we should keep changing our clothes to reflect the latest trends. For similar reasons, we may feel discouraged from releasing our self-expression.

In a world where being yourself might be seen as a radical movement, authentic expression can be life-affirming and uplifting, with positive effects for within yourself and for those around you. It doesn't have to be flashy or showy; the goal is to be yourself without the need to hide or be afraid to take up room. As a witch who relies on intuition, it's about trusting yourself to show up as *you*, no matter how hard that might be.

Within witchcraft, embodying your most entire self creates an instant rise of inner power. Physical self-expression can help us to honour the earth, celebrate the Sabbats, and enhance the tone of a ritual or ceremony. Witchcraft and Wicca emboldened me to express myself authentically, and this made me see that everything I do has power. So, when it came to decisions about tattoos, clothing and hair removal, and so on, it helped me to create a further layer of inner trust. I began to understand that the more that I expressed myself authentically, the more I enjoyed the world around me.

The consciousness needed within my Wiccan lifestyle helped me to connect my intuition to my physical appearance. I no longer felt a need to cling to an identity with draining limitations, but instead saw myself as a temple. I can collect decorations for this temple and allow change to happen as time goes on. This also helped me remove the daunting and irrelevant question of who am I supposed to be. And instead, I just started showing up as me, regardless of how I'm dressed.

## THE MAGICK IN YOUR PHYSICAL APPEARANCE

As I delved further into my Wiccan studies, I came to understand the belief that we are all a piece of this universe. Therefore, to hold on to a limiting idea of modern identity feels almost pointless.

Like stars, we exist in life and disperse in death, so for the sweet living part in the middle, we breathe, we flow and, like those heavenly bodies in the sky, we are spectacular. So, no matter how we dress, there will always be a beauty that can never disappear from us.

That said, you can harness the power of how you present yourself in the world magickally too.

# CLOTHING

When we dress ourselves every morning, we are setting an intention. When we choose our clothing and anything else that we want to wear, we can visualise what we need, what kind of energy we want to give out, or which mood we wish to create. Sometimes we might want to feel or express cosiness, confidence, creativity or reflect our imagination that day. But whatever it is, intention lies behind it – and in that case, there's magick to be created.

For me, clothes reflect my love for nature, which directly relates to Wicca and my connection with the natural world. Vintage clothing empowers me to strengthen my relationship with the environment and my need to give back instead of permanently taking from it.

If you are interested in wearing clothing for a particular purpose, have a go at piecing together an outfit on a full moon that reflects your aims. For example, if you're manifesting a personal goal that will bring you joy, try wearing colours such as orange and green that represent enjoyment. If you're manifesting passion in your love life, try wearing clothes that make *you* feel sensual.

You can also honour Sabbats with specific colours or special garments to embody what the day represents. On May Day, for example, wearing whites, florals and greens will represent fertility, new beginnings, growth and nature.

During spellwork, some people like to wear no clothing (to be 'sky clad') and to be there in their most vulnerable state to fully embody the natural connection and energy we produce in our magickal workings. However, others may want to feel comfortable and protected in their everyday loungewear. Some like to distinguish the occasion by wearing ceremonial robes or colours associated with the ritual's intention. You can also wear crystals with the specific energy that you would like to carry with you.

## TATTOOS

Tattoos are one of the most potent ways of manifesting when it comes to your appearance. Engraving an image or phrase onto your body is a symbol of where you're going and what you can expect from yourself and the universe, which is why I think it's vital to be super conscious about your choice of tattoo.

For thousands of years, tattooing has been used as a form of spiritual symbolism in many different cultures. They have been used to show status, and to distinguish people as being a part of a specific tribe or religion. Some traditional Japanese tattoos have stories behind the artwork, reflect a meaning or something that the person has experienced.

Whatever the story behind it, tattooing yourself sends a message throughout your whole being, therefore extending it to the universe. If you're interested in getting tattooed, think about setting an intention with your next choice of design, with whatever image or word you decide on. Of course, a tattoo can be something that makes you happy and feel beautiful, and that can be just as powerful as any other objective. And, obviously, they are down to personal choice – and are not for everyone.

## HAIR GROWTH – AND REMOVAL

Your hair can have magickal significance too. There are many spiritual reasons to grow your hair. Traditionally, wise women, druids and many other spiritual figures from different cultures have grown their hair to symbolise wisdom.

I believe the significance of growing or cutting hair is that it holds energy and you can choose whether to take the energy with you on your journey or whether you would like to cut it and start afresh. You can also set an intention after you've cut your hair to grow it for a certain period to signify your aims for the next period of your life. Once again, the interpretation is up to the individual.

Some people might also choose to grow their hair alongside their partner's and to weave this together during a handfasting ceremony, symbolising a voluntary, emotional bond with another person. When the hair is undone, the couple can stay together as long as they wish and with the knowledge that they have made a spiritual commitment.

Hair can be used in spellwork, usually representing a new beginning or going through a transitional stage of life. Also, as mentioned above, the simple art of expressing yourself authentically through your hair is a powerful way of honouring your inner intuition and true instincts.

## HAIR GROWTH WITH INTENTION SPELL

If you're interested in a spiritual reasoning behind hair growth, this is one for you! This specific spell is more of a manifestation.

When I first started growing my hair, my intention was simply to dedicate myself to keeping to a commitment. I grew my hair for a year and a half before entering a rough time in my life when I decided to cut it again. I had a lot of hair cut off as a need for inner transformation before I moved away from my home town, and experienced a huge ego death and shift around where I held my values. I then decided that this time I was going to grow my hair out *for me* – and I was going to love myself at every stage while doing it.

Our hair holds great power and energy, and spiritual hair growth can be done for many reasons, but setting an intention of any kind is a beautiful way to dabble in this practice, which can be very powerful and effective!

**Intent:** To set in place a major intention.

**Perfect time:** Begin any time after a haircut.

**You will need:**

a small amount of your own cut hair
pen and paper
1 small envelope
1 blue candle, great for healing and manifestation.
a wax seal stamp (*optional*)

✷ Start this ritual after you have a haircut and save some of the hair. If you are not ready for a haircut, you could always trim a tiny portion of your hair instead.

✷ Find a quiet space and set out your pen and paper, envelope, candle and your cut hair.

✷ Light the candle and start by writing your intention on a piece of paper. A general or more long-term aim, such as healing from a traumatic event, might suit this ritual due to the time it takes to grow your hair.

★ After you've finished writing, read your words out loud and then place them in the envelope along with your lock of hair.

★ Seal the envelope normally, or with a blob of candle wax and a seal. Place the sealed envelope somewhere safe, where you will be regularly reminded of your intention; in front of a mirror works well.

Experimenting magickally with your appearance can be part of finding your tribe – the people whose energies resonate with your own – so let's take a closer look next at the relationships in our lives.

# 18.

# Relationships and Friendships

Relationships and friendships are natural tides of energy that flow in and out of our lives. This is more sacred than almost any other exchange we experience. We are all connected. We are all the same, all equal and all of us share a universal energy. We do not need to be from the same background as someone to love them and we need nothing more in common than just being human to care for each other.

As I seem to keep saying, intuition and intention are of the utmost importance, and this is especially true within friendships and partnerships. We tend to know when people aren't good for us but ignore it for many reasons, including fear, nostalgia, impulse, lack of self-discipline, and trauma. This is why it's so important to take steps in relationships mindfully; and it's essential to check in with yourself regularly via meditation, divination and journaling. You can also identify aspects of unhealthy relationships by being in tune with your physical body. For example, does your heart rate accelerate when you see this person? Do you feel nervous and anxious; is it butterflies, or is it romantic attachment?

Always use your intuition as to whether a relationship feels good or dangerous, and allow yourself some time to reflect on your thoughts and feelings. If there's anything that being a witch can teach us, it's using our instincts to decide who we let into our lives. Naturally, our energies will sometimes clash and not always align with those of other people. As with the cycles that we see within our Wiccan studies, we can understand that everything runs its course. Anyone with whom we come into contact can exhibit difficult, negative or challenging behaviour and attitudes, but we can decide what we are willing to tackle and what we would prefer to keep absent from our lives.

Relationships are also easily distinguished by whether the other person is willing to collaborate with you. Are they prepared to talk about the problems and accept healthy discussions? Or are they defensive and unapologetic when you state your boundaries? Everyone has the right to live as authentically as they want, but this includes you, too. Therefore, you don't (not even for a second) have to deal with a friendship that crosses your boundaries. When you're trying to live a healthier and happier life, you may find yourself losing friends who don't have your best intentions at heart. On the other hand, we can choose not to take it personally when friendships come and go. Compassion is always the answer. Keep this thought close to you while you are coping with issues around relating to other people; this includes being compassionate to those who are struggling and also sparing yourself from harm by letting go of toxic ideals in relationships. In the long term, everyone will benefit from you removing yourself from an unhealthy connection.

## RITUAL FOR FINDING YOUR TRIBE

This spell helps attract authentic friendships and will strengthen your intuition for identifying genuine attachments instead of those that won't last. It can also lead you into a place where you are ready to make true connections, so it's worth remembering that this spell might not work instantly, so you have to trust in the process, but when it does work, it can be very powerful!

**Intent:** Attracting true friends into your life.

**Perfect time:** Best on a Friday, the weekday associated with friendship.

**You will need:**

3 pink candles in candleholders
3 flower heads (*such as daisies, roses or daffodils which evoke love, sunflowers for loyalty or sweet peas for gratitude*)

✴ Sit down and position your candles somewhere safe where they won't be disturbed or knocked over, preferably in a line in front of you. (Candle safety is essential!)

✴ Light the three candles and place the flower heads in front of them.

✴ Close your eyes and begin to visualise a pink light. Then start to imagine yourself surrounded by friends. You don't have to visualise what they look like, but attempt to picture and feel elements that you would like them to bring to your life, as well as what kind of friendships you would like to attract. You could try to feel abstract qualities, such as warmth, genuineness and creativity, and you could picture concrete objects or activities that you would like to share with others, such as plants growing in your garden, walks on the beach or dancing. Whatever feels important to you.

✴ When you've finished, open your eyes and blow out your candles.

★ Sprinkle the flower heads outside and allow your tribe to come to you.

## PROTECTING YOURSELF FROM ENERGY VAMPIRES

As well as attracting people to you, raising your vibrations can help you identify who or what it is that's draining your energy. Daily practices such as meditation, journaling and divination can all help you tune into your emotions and discover where your vitality is disappearing to. Take notice of how you feel whenever you're with someone. If you feel yourself holding back from being authentic, you are instantly blocking your heart and throat energy centres (i.e. chakras). If spending time with someone makes you feel as though you've been emotionally drained instead of uplifted, keep an eye out to see if this is a repetitive pattern when you are with them.

When it comes to manipulative energy vampires, they can be more difficult to identify. As a witch, we must always trust our intuition first. If you suspect someone might be trying to control or influence you for their own agenda, it's better to trust your instincts than to allow someone to continue to pick away at your intuition and self-worth until they disappear completely. If you are mistaken, you can always learn from this.

As witches, we have tools for divine insight that can assist us, so if you ever feel as though you're losing yourself in a relationship, platonic or otherwise, return to these tools. Divination such as tarot or scrying can help you see into your subconscious and receive psychic messages from the universe. Returning to nature can also help you to hear yourself more clearly and to make honest choices that relate to how you want to live your life. Also, protecting yourself daily with crystals and regular grounding (see 'Practical magick tip – a self-aligning

ceremony', page 122) and cleansing practices can be the perfect ways to allow yourself to think calmly and with clarity,
instead of acting impulsively.

## CLEANSING YOURSELF FROM THE
## EFFECTS OF AN ENERGY VAMPIRE

This ritual is for when you arrive back home after being around
an energy vampire. (If you'd like an in-depth cleansing ritual
for your home to clear a more potent energy or that of someone who has spent a lot of time in your house, then visit
Chapter 16, page 184.)

**Intent:** Cleansing negative energy after spending time with
an energy vampire.

**Perfect time:** When you first get home, as soon as you enter
the door.

**You will need:**

a bell of your choosing (*e.g. a Tibetan bell or a simple hand
    bell*)
incense or herb bundle of your choice (*I recommend purifying
    sage*)

✳ Hang or place the bell somewhere accessible, either just
   inside your front door or by your room door.

✳ As soon as you enter your space, ring the bell around you
   three times and take one large, deep breath.

✳ You can ring the bell an extra three times if you feel you are
   carrying additional emotional energy that day.

✳ If needed, light your incense or herb bundle and spend a
   few minutes decompressing before you start to do

anything in your space, allowing the emotional energy to melt away.

## HOW TO BREAK A NEGATIVE BOND

If energy vampires weren't enough to contend with, throughout our lives, we can frequently find ourselves caught up in negative bonds with others. Before casting a spell or working with magick, we must first take a thorough look at ourselves. More often than not, what we attract reflects where we are in our lives. If we are allowing people to drain our energy, they will continue to do so until we change something. If we don't take steps to reinforce boundaries, those people will naturally find their way in.

There is also the possibility that we have unintentionally nurtured a negative bond with someone and want to break that harmful connection; this doesn't have to mean that you want someone out of your life completely, but you might want to find a way to establish a healthy boundary between yourself and the other person.

As soon as you have the intention of breaking a bond with someone, the transition has already begun. After you've performed magickal work to complete this ending, you will be able to heal and move on.

## SPELL FOR BREAKING A HOSTILE BOND

This spell uses number magick. In numerology the number 2 represents a bond between two people, so we will use this time of the day to cut ties with a specific connection.

**Intent:** To break an emotional tie or connection with someone who has become an opposing force in your life.

**Perfect time:** Sunday or the day before the full moon for best results. The final step of this spell is to be performed at precisely 22:22; twenty-two minutes past ten in the evening.

**You will need:**

1 red candle in candleholder
1 carving tool or a thick pin, a lino-cutting tool, or even just a
    sharp pencil
red ribbon
timer
scissors

⁎ Gather the items for this spell before 22:22 to be ready to break the bonds at exactly this time.

⁎ First, take your red candle and carve the initials of the person that you would like to break bonds with.

⁎ Place your candle in the candleholder and tie the red ribbon around the centre of the candle.

⁎ Burn this candle for 2 minutes, starting at exactly 22:20. Set your timer.

⁎ When the timer reaches 22:22, blow out the candle immediately and cut the ribbon with your scissors. Once you have done this, say the words:

*I cut all negative ties with [name of the person] from now until the end.
Allow me to heal and lift this emotional weight from my shoulders. So mote it be.*

⁎ After this spell, the bond will be broken and you will begin to heal. You may still feel emotions concerning this person, but, as you have cut all negative ties, the universe can now let healing take place.

By freeing yourself up from the bonds that are tying you down in unhelpful ways, you will allow more space for positive energy to flow into and through your life. Of course, a wonderful source of supportive energy can be found all around us – in nature.

# 19.

# Magick Outside

In the last chapter of this book, I want to talk about how we can work magickally with the earth around us. As we all know, Wicca is a nature-based religion that primarily focuses on worship of and consideration for the natural world and the part that we play on this wonderful earth during our practices. As a long-term practitioner, I had been under the misapprehension that to be a 'true' Wiccan, you should ideally live in the countryside; obviously, this turned out to be false. I have loved being surrounded by nature during times throughout my life and found it wonderful to be so close to woods, rivers and wildlife. However, since moving to a city, I realised that, regardless of where you live, you can connect with nature, even if it's simply of the human kind.

During the last couple of years, I have lived in four different homes, each in different locations. I have found that I developed a different way of working with nature depending on whether I was living in a rural village, a small market town, or a city, and have found beautiful ways to connect with each place, regardless of how much 'greenery' there is around me.

The reality is that many of us live in built-up towns or cities; you just need an open mind and the ability to find magick wherever you are based. I think we need to be available to work with all elements of the universe. You can practise spellcraft everywhere and anywhere you want if you search hard enough!

So, in this chapter, there are eight spells inspired by each of the four places I have lived in over the last few years – the country-side, towns, small cities and large cities – embracing nature in the elements that each climate gave to me.

## WILD FLOWER CLEANSING

This is a fun and straightforward cleansing bundle that encourages you to get outside and go foraging for some wild flowers. As for all of these spells, feel free to use your intuition about which flowers you pick and add to your bunch! However, please don't take all the flowers you find, uproot them or pick plants that are endangered. Leave some of the flowers for others to enjoy too. If you are unsure what a plant is, it's always worth looking it up before picking it or handling it.

The purpose of this bundle is to raise your vibrations whenever you feel the need. All of the flowers and herbs suggested below are great for attracting joy and cleansing negative emotions away!

**Inspired by:** Rural country living.

**Intent:** Raising your vibrations.

**Perfect time:** Late springtime, early summer.

**You will need:**

a couple of rosemary sprigs
1 handful of cornflowers
1 handful of cow parsley
1 handful of elderflower heads
1 handful of daisies
yarn or string
lighter or matches

* Go out and forage responsibly for your flowers. You may need to buy some fresh rosemary if you can't find any out in the wild, or you could substitute it with a different herb such as thyme. (Remember not to harvest all the plants you find, but leave some for others to enjoy.)

* Once you have collected all of your flowers and herbs, take them home and dry them.

* It might be easier to tie all of your flowers together in a bundle before you dry them, to ensure that they don't fall apart. If you are using fresh flowers to burn with sprigs of dried herbs, collect these later and add them when you want to burn the bundle.

* Assemble your bundle of dried plant material using your yarn or string, adding in any fresh flowers by tucking them into the thread. Tie the yarn at intervals along the bundle and trim so that all of the stems are the same length.

* Burn this bundle while dancing in a circle, moving it around you a few times to raise your vibrations!

* After doing this, put out the burning carefully and hang the bundle somewhere, ready to reuse when you next need a vibration boost!

## WARM ELDERFLOWER CORDIAL FOR EMOTIONAL CLEARING

Making and drinking this cordial is a wonderfully positive experience for anytime that you have had a long or tough day. When we came out of lockdown in the UK, and I was suddenly surrounded by other people's energy after a long period of only having to deal with my own – I found myself stressed and overwhelmed – and this drink was invaluable for me then.

Elderflower can be found growing in the wild in the UK from the end of May to the middle of June, so be sure to do your research before choosing to do this spell, and don't confuse this shrub with cow parsley! Harvest the flower heads away from busy roads wherever possible to avoid pollution.

Elderflower is a protection and purification plant used throughout witchcraft for several purposes, including in cleansing herb bundles (see above). If you know you're going to have a long day, keep this cordial at hand to mix with some boiling water for the perfect, calming drink!

**Inspired by:** Rural country living.

Intent: To clear your energy after an emotionally testing day.

**Perfect time:** Whenever elderflowers are in season.

**You will need:**

20 elderflower heads (the bigger, the better!)
3 sliced lemons
1kg (2lb) sugar
50g (2oz) citric acid
1.5l (2.5pt) water
sterilised bottle(s) with a screw-up top
label(s) and pen

**To make the cordial:**

✶ Go out and pick your elderflower heads. Take them home and check them for bugs. I would recommend not rinsing the elderflowers excessively; instead just remove the bugs and give them a gentle rinse here and there if needed.

* Add your elderflowers, lemon, sugar, citric acid and water to a large pan. Heat and stir until it reaches boiling point. Then simmer on a low heat for 5 minutes.

* Leave the elderflower mixture to cool overnight.

* The following day, drain your mixture through a cheese-cloth or sieve.

* Once finished, store the cordial in sterilised glass bottles. Label these with the name of the cordial and the date on which you made it. The cordial should keep in the fridge for up to a month.

**The spell:**

* Pour a small amount of cordial into a mug followed by some hot water and top it up with cold water if needed.

* Take your spoon and stir anticlockwise three times to repel negative energy.

* Drink slowly and feel the wave of emotional energy leave you.

## LISTEN TO THE TREES

When I feel a sense of longing, I turn to the trees for my truth. The trees help show us that the truth is inside us already and they hold a certain wisdom that we can't easily possess as humans.

Take a walk amongst the trees nearby and find a flow in your steps. Maybe take a look at the sky as you move and notice the patterns and shapes up above you, which we rarely observe. You may already hear the trees chatting, bringing thoughts, questions, scenarios and answers. You might have a question in mind for them, such as asking whether you should leave behind something that no longer serves you or if you should chase that desire of yours.

The trees point out the perfection in simplicity and the beauty in imperfections. They might tell you to take a break, focus on your soul, and let go of your ego. They may call you to spend more time with them and to come to visit them in the mornings. They may ask you to love and delve deeper into awareness or meditation.

**Inspired by:** Town living.

Intent: To gain clarity on a situation or gain some emotional space to decide your next move.

Perfect time: Anytime that you feel a sense of emotional confusion or uncertainty over a situation.

You will need: A quiet place to walk where there are trees, such as a park or other wooded area.

⁎ When you are looking for answers and unable to find a way forwards, go to the trees, sit with them and chant:

> *Ground, you are my home,*
> *the sky, you are my calling,*
> *the sun, you are my needs,*
> *pond, you are my flow,*
> *now heart, answer my prayer.*

⁎ Recognise what comes to mind after this calling, note it down, and act accordingly. These are the answers that you are seeking.

# BLACKBERRY JAM MANIFESTATION SPELL

Blackberries are a delicious fruit that can be found growing wild in hedgerows, gardens and wasteland, usually around mid to late August in Britain. Blackberries can be used for many things, especially spells surrounding prosperity. The branches can be hung in your home and used for protection.

This spell can manifest something in a short period or for the future. A few years ago, I picked some blackberries and used them to manifest some money when I was running a little short! Jam making, to me, is mainly done by observing and intuition, so you may want to add more or less sugar, depending on how you like the texture and taste of your jam.

**Inspired by:** Town living.

**Intent:** To manifest something that you need; this can be an affirmation of a feeling such as 'joy' or something more tangible.

**Perfect time:** Anytime that you can get hold of some blackberries!

**You will need:**

600g (1¼lb) blackberries
400g (14oz) caster sugar
3 tbsp lemon juice
3 sterilised jam jars
pen and labels
piece of yarn
incense (*the scent should relate to your manifestation, e.g., sandalwood for money, rose for love.*)

★ Go out and pick some blackberries. Take your time and enjoy yourself!

★ Place your blackberries in a large saucepan with the sugar, bring to boil, and then simmer for around 30 minutes until the fruit has really softened.

★ Turn the heat up to medium until the jam thickens.

★ Add the lemon juice, give it a stir, taste for sweetness and leave to cool.

★ You can always add other flavouring, such as ginger for calmness if you want to experiment.

★ Place your jam into your jar once cooled.

★ Write your manifestation on a label and tie it around the jar. Seal it with a lid and circle some lit incense around the outside of the jar, repeating your manifestation aloud three times.

★ You can put different manifestations on different jars and use them at times when you need them.

★ After this, eat the jam and use it for other recipes to strengthen the manifestations! The jam can be stored in a cool, dry place for up to 12 months and, once opened, will keep in the fridge for around 4 weeks.

## FEATHER DIVINATION

Feather divination is not a common practice within witchcraft but, nevertheless, it's very effective. It stems from the belief in age-old folklore that finding a feather can mean different things to each individual. You might have heard that if you see a white feather, it means the spirit of a loved one or your angels are looking over you. But we can add to this magick by expanding our knowledge of what certain feathers can mean to us and relate to where we currently are in life. This knowledge isn't a new practice and versions of it can be found throughout many cultures. The knack is to use the information to make choices within your life and to interpret finding a feather as a signal to make the moves towards whatever you wish for.

The following list is based on my recordings of the meanings of feathers that have appeared in my life over the last five years. I've only been gifted a pink feather once and found an indigo one once, too, so I would encourage you to follow your intuition and use this as a guideline for your own divination practice. When you're on a walk, remember to keep an eye out for feathers. If you spot one randomly, even better! The practice can also include spotting synthetically dyed feathers.

**Inspired by:** Small city living.

Intent: To interpret feathers as signs and act on these.

Perfect time: Notice them simply when walking and being present without any distractions.

## BLACK FEATHERS

- *Meaning:* Black can indicate a shift or change coming into your life, mainly an ending to something, and it will be happening soon. This may be positive or negative, but either way, expect some significant changes.

- *Message:* Protect your energy during this time, cleanse as much as you are able and meditate to keep balance.

## WHITE FEATHERS

- **Meaning:** White indicates clarity and calm. But you may also find that things are a little too still.

- **Message:** It's time to make plans, because soon you will need to start *doing*. You are in the right place, and the world is ready to give you what you have wished for.

## BLUE OR TEAL FEATHERS

- **Meaning:** This colour commonly indicates healing and, more importantly, the value of recovery in your life right now.

- **Message:** If you are not actively looking after yourself and your needs, it's time to start settling down and focusing on your healing journey. Take a step back and concentrate on that part of your life for a while.

## RED FEATHERS

- **Meaning:** This is an extremely unique feather, and if you find one, it's a warning from the divine. There will be a force coming into your life soon that may either be overwhelmingly negative or positive. Either way, it will knock you off your feet and leave you changed.

- **Message:** It's time to protect yourself, but keep going. From what I've learnt after finding this feather twice, the upcoming experience can't be stopped, only minimalised to keep you balanced. However, if you wish to find stability during this time, listen to the warning. Whether it means taking some alone time in nature or welcoming more home comforts into your life, try to find something that will keep you grounded during whatever is coming.

## GREY FEATHERS

- **Meaning:** Grey-coloured feathers mean peace is on the horizon, so don't give up yet!

- **Message:** Things may currently feel hopeless or overwhelming, but this feather tells you to keep moving forward a little longer because harmony or self-acceptance is coming soon.

## BROWN FEATHERS

- **Meaning:** Brown indicates home and grounding.

- **Message:** It's time to find your feet and settle down for a while. You may feel the need to start nesting in soon, for whatever reason.

## GREEN FEATHERS OR WITH A GREENISH TINT

- **Meaning:** Growth is on the cards, either in your career, financially, personally or in a goal or manifestation that you've set!

- **Message:** Whatever you are doing right now, you're doing it right! If you have any plans that you want to set in place, take action and push for your aspirations; the rewards are coming to you!

## YELLOW FEATHERS OR WITH YELLOW MARKINGS

- **Meaning:** You will soon be surrounded with joy and energy, so now is the time to use that vitality and fun to get the most out of life!

- **Message:** You can use this time to appreciate what's going on around you, but if you have anything that needs doing, make use of this energy!

## PURPLE OR INDIGO

- **Meaning:** A message from the divine is coming, resulting in spiritual transformation and growth!

- **Message:** You may be about to experience a turbulent or an exciting time. Either way, it's coming – and my advice would be to allow this. Nothing to be done or changed!

## PINK

- **Meaning:** Love is coming, or the love in your life is what you need right now.

- **Message:** Whether you have met someone or have an abundance of self-love, this will fill you with hope and healing. If you haven't met someone or are planning to stay single, this could indicate brilliant friendships or the necessity of a strong awareness of self-value.

## MIXED COLOUR FEATHERS

- **Meaning:** A mixed-coloured feather can indicate confusion or being lost, away from your path. It's time to get back onto the right track and examine your priorities!

- **Message:** Get your head straight before manifesting your goals or making any big decisions. It could help if you work out what you want before jumping into making plans or working towards something new.

# SIGIL WATER SPELL FOR BANISHING A PROBLEM

This spell is easy and quick, but powerful to use when you have an ongoing problem in your life that you would like to bring to a close soon. It involves some nature and sigil magick and the powerful cleansing abilities of natural water to assist you with your intentions. Use this spell when you are confident that the time is right to bring this problem to an end and when you are prepared to deal with any after-effects of this closure.

**Inspired by:** Small city living.

**Intent:** To banish an ongoing issue in life.

**Perfect time:** Waning moon would be the most effective, or on a Thursday or Saturday.

**You will need:**

1 jar with a lid
1 small pebble
paint that isn't water-resistant
a thin paintbrush

★ Take a walk somewhere near open water and bring your jar with you. Choose your body of water depending on your connection with the place or the form of water, and what water sources are available to you. For example, if you feel at peace by the sea, or have a favourite spot by a river or pond, choose accordingly.

★ Fill your jar up to the top with your chosen water and fasten the lid.

* Find a small pebble or rock and take your jar of water and pebble home.

* On the appropriate day for the spellwork, paint your pebble with this sigil:

Then allow it to dry.

* On the other side of your pebble, write ONE WORD that represents your issue; in order to direct the focus of the universe to this. It can be a name, a feeling, or just a word associated with the problem.

* Leave the paint to dry for a short while, then place the pebble in your jar of water and seal it.

* Leave it under the moon either outside or indoors on a windowsill to charge for one evening. After that, keep the jar in your room until the sigil has washed away or until your scenario has come to a close.

* After your problem has cleared, pour the water into the ground with the pebble, to return it to the earth.

## TO LET GO OF WORRYING THOUGHTS

When I'm worried or anxious, I like to walk alone in nature and allow it to ground me. Even when I am in a city, I seek out natural features such as rivers and parks. A few years ago, I was strolling near my favourite river, full of anxiety, when I spotted a large stone that was seemingly jumping out at me. It had red and white speckles on it and it felt solid and smooth. I picked up the stone, took it home, washed it until it was clean, and decided it would be a worry stone. So, I carry this around whenever I feel anxious to help pull my thoughts down to earth and ground me.

**Inspired by:** City living.

**Intent:** To create a worry stone.

**Perfect time:** Anytime you have worrying or overwhelming thoughts. A full moon is particularly powerful for working this spell.

**You will need:**

1 medium-sized stone
thin paintbrush and paint

* Go for a walk and take some time to breathe, even if you feel overrun with mind traffic.

* Have a look around and find a medium-sized stone that seemingly stands out to you. Try not to overthink your choice and trust your intuition when you feel that you've found one which could suit your purpose.

* Go home and wash the stone. Make sure it's really clean. You can also cleanse the stone with some smoke, much like you would a crystal.

* Grab some paint and a fine paintbrush. I often choose the colour blue for this spell as it's a healing colour that can help calm anxiety. Then paint the calming sigil below (or your own) onto the stone:

This sigil roughly translates to 'a quieter, peaceful, mind'. It will help activate the positive intention of the worry stone.

✶ After this, leave the stone to dry overnight. If you'd like, you can place it under a full moon to raise its vibrations or recharge when it needs it later!

✶ Then whenever you have worry or anxiety, carry the stone with you or hold the stone for a few seconds to help calm and quieten your mind.

## TO LET GO OF A PAINFUL PAST SCENARIO

For me, water has always been a healing element. Even though I have no water signs in my chart, nor am I a water witch, nature swimming and bathing have always been a form of healing and a spiritual release.

This ritual is to be performed when you are genuinely ready to move on from a scenario that hurt you. Of course, this doesn't mean the pain won't flare up again, but you're letting the universe know that you're ready to move past your troubles.

**Inspired by:** City living (specifically Brighton).

**Purpose:** To let go of something in preparation for moving on.

**Perfect time:** Best performed on a new moon, a Sunday or a day that is relevant to the situation (see 'Weekdays', page 13).

**You will need:**

a shell (*bring this with you if necessary*)

small towel or flannel (*anything that will soak up a small amount of water will do!*)
a sharpie, a pen, or a small amount of acrylic paint and a brush

*Optional extras:*
flask of hot drink and snack
towel or blanket to sit on

* Head to a beach, lake or other watercourse that has exceptionally safe energy for you.

* If it's cold, get warm and cosy, and be sure to wear something comfortable. I like to bring a flask of coffee or tea and something to eat with me when I know I'm dealing with something slightly heavier.

* Set yourself up near the water, and lay down a towel or blanket if you wish somewhere dry.

* Look around your safe space for a shell that's big enough to draw on. If you are not near a beach, you will need to plan ahead and bring a shell with you for this ritual. Make sure you wash it thoroughly and pat it dry with a towel or flannel.

* Take your paint or pen and paint this sigil on it:

It represents your pain, and once it's thrown into the water, it translates to active healing. You can, of course, choose another sigil for this if you want to, but mine is here if you need it.

* Allow this to dry for a few minutes. While you're doing this, close your eyes and take in the noises and your surroundings. Try to imagine your pain disappearing into the water, floating away, never to be felt again. If you're near the ocean, you can imagine the sea taking the pain away, wave by wave.

* Enjoy the clarity for a few minutes and once you're ready, walk up to the water and throw your shell into the sea, river, lake or stream. Enjoy the force of throwing it into the water, as it disappears forever.

* Inhale some deep breaths and stay near the water as long as you like to take the time to reflect.

# Final Words

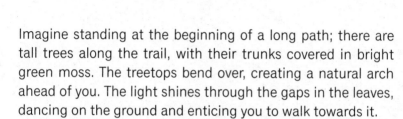

Imagine standing at the beginning of a long path; there are tall trees along the trail, with their trunks covered in bright green moss. The treetops bend over, creating a natural arch ahead of you. The light shines through the gaps in the leaves, dancing on the ground and enticing you to walk towards it.

Now, imagine yourself as the most whole version of yourself, embracing all of your natural flaws. You have healed from anything that weighs on your soul. You know who you are in a more profound sense than just being about others' perception of you, or how valuable you feel to those around you. You are more than your thoughts, more than your emotions, more than your reactions. You are whole, and as you walk forwards a light begins to shine from within you – it becomes brighter and more radiant and you become aware that this path will be a lifelong journey. You will feel more at peace day by day, year by year, for all eternity, as your soul is eternal and will forever be a part of the universe until the end of time.

Life is not about permanent progression but the ability to stay open to growth. No matter who you are now and what you feel needs to change, you have everything you need inside to grow into the fullest version of yourself.

Understanding and learning about nature, witchcraft and meditation have continuously helped me understand myself and my purpose. I hope that whatever you get out of this book, you find peace and a way to be at home within yourself, regardless of whatever is happening around you. If you choose to connect to yourself and the earth around you, you will have a beautiful journey ahead of you. Believe in magick, believe in your intuition and be gentle with yourself along the way.

# Resources

## BOOKS

Julia Cameron, *The Artist's Way*, Souvenir Press, 2020

Scott Cunningham, *Living Wicca: A Guide for the Solitary Practitioner*, Llewellyn, 1989

Jack Kornfield, *The Wise Heart: Buddhist Psychology for the West*, Rider Books, 2008

Harmony Nice, *Wicca: A Modern Guide to Witchcraft & Magick*, Orion Spring, 2018 (my first book)

Harmony Nice, *The Harmony Tarot: A Deck for Growth and Healing*, Rider Books, 2021 (my tarot deck)

Sarah Prout, *Dear Universe: 200 Mini Meditations for Instant Manifestations*, Piatkus, 2019

Moonwater SilverClaw, *The Goddess Has Your Back: How Wicca Can Help You Raise Your Self-Esteem and Make Your Life Magickal*, QuickBreakthrough Publishing, 2014

## WEBSITES

**goddessandgreenman.co.uk** – Perfect for all the basic Wiccan principles and how to get started in your craft.

**www.thehoodwitch.com** – An excellent blog that dives deeply into all things witchcraft and magick-related.

**www.wiccadaily.com** – A place to find information on Wicca, spellwork news and helpful tips for your journey.

**www.witchfest.net** – A large organisation that will help you find witchcraft and Wicca-based events nearby.

# PODCASTS

**The Fat Feminist Witch podcast** – Hosted by Paige Vanderbeck, this podcast is a fresh, appealing approach to witchcraft. This podcast gets down into the nitty-gritty of spellwork, social media magick, and body love.

**Heart Wisdom with Jack Kornfield** – Though this isn't a Wiccan or witchcraft-based podcast, Jack's wisdom and common sense can inspire anyone on any branch of spirituality to help heal and grow.

**The Queer Witch podcast** – Anna Joy takes a sweet approach to discussing queerness within our crafts and tarot, self-care, and manifesting. The queer witch podcast is an insightful podcast for those that want to have fun and learn.

**Tending the Flame with Brónach & Denise** – Brónach and Denise take a hilarious and approachable point of view to discuss spirituality. They have many discussions on witchcraft, Wicca, feminism, and sexuality, all informative and a joy to listen to.

**Witches of Atlanta podcast** – Hosted by three lovely witches, with informative conversations around feminism, race, sex, love and reclaiming your power.

# SHOPS

**BehatiLife Apothecary**
www.behatilife.com

**Gaia's Magick**
29 Sydney St, Brighton BN1 4EP

**The Hoodwitch**
www.thehoodwitch.com

**Wicca Daily**
www.wiccadaily.com

**Every Witch Way**
www.everywitchway.co.uk

# Acknowledgements

I would like to thank everyone that has supported me, whether it be on YouTube, Instagram, or by purchasing my books or from my jewellery collections over the last seven years. You may have just picked up this book on a whim or as a long-term follower of my work, but your support has been life-changing, and I will always appreciate it. The journey that I have taken to tell my story, educate my audience on the Wiccan faith and keeping virtual company of so many amazing people will continue to change and transition as I navigate the next chapters in my life.

I would also like to thank the team at Penguin Random House, including Olivia, Liz and everyone else who worked so hard to make this book possible.

A special thanks to my family: Mum, Dad, Bella and Vivi. My friends for supporting me and the fellow members of the Wiccan and witchcraft community for making the world a more magickal place.

# About the Author

Harmony Nice is an author and Wiccan practitioner. She became interested in witchcraft and Wicca at the age of fourteen after discovering that her great-grandmother Hilda was a witch. Three years later she started her YouTube channel to communicate with other practitioners, educate newcomers and generate discussion about Wicca, magick and spirituality. Her first book, *Wicca*, was published in 2018 and *The Harmony Tarot: A Deck for Growth and Healing* was published in 2021. She is currently based in Brighton, UK.

# Notes

NOTES

238

NOTES